The Psychological Contract in the Public Sector

ONE WEEK LOAN

David E. Gues

Neil Conway

The Chartered Institute of Personnel and Development is the leading publisher of books and reports for personnel and training professionals, students, and all those concerned with the effective management and development of people at work. For full details of all our titles, please contact the Publishing Department:

Tel: 020 8263 3387
Fax: 020 8263 3850

E-mail: publish@cipd.co.uk

The catalogue of all CIPD titles can be viewed on the CIPD website:
www.cipd.co.uk/publications

The Psychological Contract in the Public Sector

The Results of the 2000 CIPD Survey of the Employment Relationship

David E. Guest
The Management Centre, King's College, London

Neil Conway
School of Management and Organisational Psychology
Birkbeck College, University of London

First published 2000

Cover design by Curve
Designed and typeset by Beacon GDT
Printed in Great Britain by Short Run Press

British Library Cataloguing in Publication Data
A catalogue record for this book is available from the British Library

ISBN 0 85292 892 0

Chartered Institute of Personnel and Development,
CIPD House, Camp Road, London SW19 4UX

Tel: 020 8971 9000
Fax: 020 8263 3333
Website: www.cipd.co.uk

Incorporated by Royal Charter. Registered charity no. 1079797.

Contents

Acknowledgements

The CIPD acknowledges the contribution of the Centre for Management and Policy Studies (CMPS), and the assistance of Ewart Wooldridge, Director of the Civil Service College directorate of CMPS.

Foreword

Over the last two decades, a succession of initiatives has been undertaken to extend the operation of business disciplines and practices within the public sector. Next steps agencies, market-testing, best value, modernising government, the NHS Plan – the underlying assumption in each case is that the public sector should be managed more like the private sector. There are some limits imposed by the nature of political accountability, even if it is sometimes difficult to be clear what those limits are; but the general trend has been towards an increased blurring of the boundaries. This raises an interesting question about the way in which people working in the public and private sectors feel about their work. For example, do employees in both sectors display similar levels of satisfaction and commitment, or do significant differences remain between them on these and other dimensions?

Recognising the critical importance of employee commitment to delivering improved business performance, individual employers in both public and private sectors have in recent years made increasing use of employee attitude surveys. In some cases, employee responses now feature in the appraisal of senior managers' performance. Attitude surveys can also be an important way of tracking the changing nature of the employment relationship across the UK labour force as a whole. This is why the Chartered Institute of Personnel and Development (CIPD) has undertaken a series of annual surveys of employee attitudes on a national basis, and reports on these surveys have continued to monitor the state of the 'psychological contract' between employers and employees.

In view of the scale of changes under way, the CIPD decided this year to explore in more detail employee attitudes in central government, local government and healthcare, so as to be able to compare the situation in these three sectors as well as between the public and private sectors as a whole. This meant doubling the size of the sample, so as to be certain that the findings were robust. The survey was developed in consultation with national employer bodies in each sector and with financial support from central and local government. It is encouraging that, in both local government and the NHS, individual employing bodies are now either required or encouraged to conduct their own surveys. This report provides national-level information that will offer a useful benchmark against which individual employers can assess the results for their own organisation.

Key findings

Previous research undertaken for the CIPD shows that human resource practices have a powerful positive effect on employee attitudes and on performance, and that this effect is achieved largely through the medium of a positive 'psychological contract'. This report shows that the public sector has adopted a larger number of people management practices than the private sector, confirming the findings of the recent Workplace Employee Relations Survey (WERS 1998). There is also more scope for employees to participate in day-to-day decisions about their work in the public sector. However, we know that the number of human resource practices in the public sector is not associated with a range of outcomes in the way that is evident in the private sector.

The present study shows that remarkably, despite reporting more practices in support of fair treatment and employee well-being, employees in central government have a poorer psychological contract than employees in any of the other three sectors. Taken as a whole, employees in central government also report: lower levels of commitment and satisfaction; less trust in management; a less dynamic, creative and friendly climate in the workplace; a less positive work–life balance; more promises by management that have not been kept; and lower satisfaction with life in general. Employees in the healthcare sector, on the other hand, are generally the most satisfied and report higher levels of motivation and effort.

What is the explanation for the low scores in central government? Survey findings of this kind can take us only so far towards an answer and it will be primarily for the management of individual departments and agencies to consider the significance of these findings. However, the data do offer a number of clues about the nature of the problem. Central government employees are less inclined than those in other sectors to show high levels of trust in their employer: the percentage reporting a willingness to trust senior management to look after their best interests 'a lot' is only about half that in other sectors. This is *not* a problem with attitudes towards individual line managers, who enjoy broadly the same high level of trust across all sectors: it is an issue to do with attitudes towards the *organisation as a whole*.

One obvious reason why trust in senior management is so low in central government is clearly the finding that employees feel less fairly treated than in any other sector. Despite consistently positive readings for the psychological contract as a whole, significant proportions of employees across the workforce generally believe that management promises – with respect for example to job security and equal treatment – have not been fully kept. However, employees in central government are less convinced than those in other sectors that promises they believe have been made to them have been kept.

Why is this so? We might speculate that the shift away from centralised employment systems, the adoption of tighter frameworks for managing performance and the difficulty of identifying any longer a distinct 'public service' ethos may all have contributed to feelings of dissatisfaction. The reasons motivating people to go into these jobs may not now be valued. There may be a particular problem in central government to do with the centralised nature of financial and political accountability and the impact this has on the ability of managers down the line to take the initiative in addressing specific problems. There may also be an issue about the nature of promises or commitments made in central government, which are perhaps more likely than those in other sectors to be subject to change or targeted at more than one audience. Whatever the explanation, however, employees in central government clearly believe that management is not keeping its side of the bargain.

The report shows a widespread sense of unfairness with respect to the effort–reward bargain in general, and pay in particular. Although this is strongest in central government, it applies across the other sectors also. However, the critical issue is how far employees believe they are being fairly treated, and there is no evidence to suggest that pay levels in themselves are key to improving the psychological contract. It seems more plausible to believe that such improvement needs to be sought through addressing the 'softer' issues highlighted in this report. There may, for example, be scope for extending levels of direct participation among junior staff in central government. The items on organisational climate shown in Table 3 also provide considerable food for thought by public sector managers: for example, nearly two out of three employees in central government believe the cultural climate of their organisation is 'constraining' – significantly more than in any other sector. Only one in three believes it is 'dynamic' and slightly more than two out of five say it is 'creative'.

Within central government, more employees now work in agencies or non-departmental organisations of one kind or another than in traditional departments of state. This raises the interesting question whether the experience of working for an agency differs significantly from that of working in a department. The philosophy underpinning the establishment of 'next steps' agencies was to enable the activities for which they were responsible to be managed more effectively at arms' length from central government. Surprisingly, however, the report finds few differences in attitudes between agencies and departments. Agency employees are more committed and report putting in more effort; employees in central departments are more motivated. There are, however, no other significant differences in attitudes, nor are there any significant differences in human resource practices between agencies and departments. This might suggest that the momentum established by the launch of 'next steps' agencies in the late 1980s has now been largely spent.

Public interest has increasingly focused on issues about long hours and the balance between work and other aspects of life. One conclusion from the report is that, in the public sector in particular, workload and work demands are leading to long hours of work, though for some this reflects their own choice. Three out of four people across the workforce as a whole say they have the right balance between work and life outside work, and there is little significant variation between sectors. However, looking at satisfaction with life, and with individual aspects of life outside work, employees in central government report lower levels of satisfaction than the other three groups, while employees in healthcare are more satisfied in all respects. Since there is a strong association between life satisfaction and the state of the psychological contract, it seems that action to improve employees' experience of work would be likely to have beneficial effects for their lives as a whole, including their health and relationships with family and friends.

Conclusion

These findings will have considerable interest, not only for people working in the public sector and those responsible for its management, but for anybody interested in the employment relationship and how it can be managed more effectively. The CIPD will be discussing with employer bodies in central and local government and in the National Health Service whether they would see value in conducting surveys of this kind in future years, and how far this would help in providing a wider context in which to interpret the findings of employer-based surveys.

Meanwhile, there is much for public sector managers to ponder in this report. One broad message is the importance of focusing on people management and development, as much as on finance and other resources, if there is a wish to improve standards of public sector management. Higher levels of public service will surely not be delivered by a disaffected workforce. A second message is that employees have high expectations of work in the public sector and, despite the evident difficulties, it would be well worth making bigger efforts to manage those expectations. There are no simple answers, but one final message is that without a basis for mutual trust and confidence, employees are unlikely to display continuing high levels of commitment.

Mike Emmott

Adviser, Employee Relations
Chartered Institute of Personnel and Development

Executive summary

- The report presents the findings of a survey of 2,000 workers, 500 in central government, 500 in local government, 500 in the health sector and 500 in private industry. The survey explores workers' perceptions of their current employment relationship, based on the concept of the psychological contract. It is part of an annual series of surveys on the employment relationship conducted by the CIPD. The responses were obtained through telephone interviews.

- More 'progressive' human resource practices are in place in the public sector, and more particularly in central government, than in the private sector. Out of a list of 11 practices, central government workers report that on average 8.2 are in place, compared with 5.9 in private industry.

- A core finding is that workers in central government, whilst reporting the presence of the widest range of positive HR policies and practices, are the least satisfied with their employment relationship. Health sector workers are the most content.

- 91 per cent in the sample report that their organisation actively carries out equal opportunity practices and 81 per cent say their organisation takes active steps to prevent people like them from being harassed and bullied at work. These figures are much higher in the public than in the private sector. They call into question claims that organisations are being slow to respond to concerns about harassment and bullying at work.

- Public sector workers report more control over their day-to-day work than workers in the private sector. However, level in the organisation is a more important determinant of control over work than sector.

- Workers in the public sector describe their organisations as more bureaucratic and less dynamic than those in the private sector. Private sector workers view their organisations as less ethical and less public-spirited.

- Central government employees believe that their organisation has made more promises to them but has kept fewer of them than workers in other sectors.

- Two out of five workers do not feel that they are fairly rewarded for the effort they put into their jobs. Workers in the private sector are more likely to feel that they are fairly treated than those in the public sector and more particularly those in central government. Over half of the central government workers believe they are not fairly paid.

- A positive psychological contract, reflected in fair treatment, delivery of promises and trust in management, is strongly linked to corporate policy and practice, especially more human resource practices, more direct participation and a more friendly and dynamic climate. Despite experiencing these, central government workers report a significantly poorer psychological contract than other workers, suggesting some more fundamental concerns.

- 43 per cent of workers report a high level of satisfaction with work and only 9 per cent report a very low level.

- Health sector workers report the highest level of satisfaction with work and commitment to their organisation while central government workers report lower levels of both satisfaction and commitment.

- Workers believe that although they show loyalty to the organisation, this is not reciprocated. By implication, workers attribute any lack of commitment to the organisation rather than themselves.

- Job insecurity is not a problem. Only 13 per cent say they feel either 'fairly' or 'very' insecure. Central government workers feel most secure.

- 86 per cent say they feel very or fairly motivated in their job and 55 per cent look forward to going to work when they wake up in the morning, either all the time or most of the time. These people are also satisfied with their work. They are more likely to be found in local government or the health sector than in central government or industry.

- Men report that they work less hard and feel less obliged to be good citizens of their organisation than women.

- Central government workers report a poorer psychological contract and are the most dissatisfied and disaffected, although they are the least likely to be thinking of leaving the organisation.

- 14 per cent work more than 48 hours a week; twice as many do this in the private sector as in the public sector. More in the private sector do this out of personal choice – 55 per cent compared with 33 per cent in the health sector.

- An extensive set of family-friendly practices are in place in the public sector and especially in central government. There are fewer in industry. The use of family-friendly practices is associated with a less satisfactory work–life balance.

- 74 per cent say they have the right balance between work and the rest of their lives. Those least likely to report the right balance are those working long hours and those who are part of management, as well as women and those with dependent children.

- 60 per cent say they are equally committed to work and to life outside work. Only 14 per cent say that work is their dominant central life interest. However, most accept that work cannot be kept separate from the rest of life and about half said that work can get in the way of life outside work.

- Satisfaction with life as a whole is generally high – and higher than satisfaction with work. Satisfaction is lowest with respect to personal finances relatively speaking. Workers in central government report the lowest levels of satisfaction with all aspects of life.

- 55 per cent said their organisation had gone through some sort of major change in the last year. More change was reported by those working in central government (65 per cent) than those in the private sector (48 per cent). Central government has placed emphasis on culture change and related activities.

◘ Change generally has a negative impact on attitudes and behaviour. The more change, the greater the negative impact. At the same time, different types of change have different impacts. Redundancies and staff cut-backs had a particularly negative impact on those who stayed with the organisation, while team-building had a more positive impact.

◘ The changes most desired by workers themselves reflect a conventional agenda. 29 per cent want improved pay and benefits, 11 per cent want a reduced workload and shorter hours and 9 per cent want promotion/advancement.

◘ Compared with previous years, responses in 2000 have changed only slightly. However, there is a significant improvement in scores on life satisfaction between 1998 and 2000, which is one indication of a general improvement in well-being.

1 | Introduction

◘ **The 2000 survey focuses in particular on the psychological contract in the public sector and the issue of work–life balance**

◘ **In this context, the psychological contract can be defined as, 'The perception of both parties to the employment relationship, organisation and individual, of the reciprocal promises and obligations implied in that relationship.'**

For the last six years, the Chartered Institute of Personnel and Development (CIPD) has been conducting a survey of employees' views about the state of the employment relationship. As trade union membership has fallen to about 30 per cent of the working population and as the proportion of workers covered by collective bargaining has declined, it has become important to understand the contemporary employment relationship in terms of a rather different framework. These surveys have used the concept of the psychological contract.

The psychological contract can be defined for present purposes as 'the perceptions of both parties to the employment relationship, organisation and individual, of the reciprocal promises and obligations implied in that relationship'. The value of the psychological contract lies partly in its recognition of the individualisation of the employment relationship. It can usefully be understood as an individual–organisation relationship, although this raises interesting questions about who or what represents the organisation in the mind of the employee. A second advantage of this perspective is that it focuses on the concerns of individual employees while allowing contextual factors such as company policy and any union role to shape individual attitudes and behaviour. It is important to bear in mind that it is a *psychological* contract; it is therefore based on the subjective perceptions of workers (or agents of the organisation).

However, it is these perceptions that can be crucial in shaping related attitudes and behaviour at work.

One of the reasons for the growing interest in the concept of the psychological contract is a widespread belief that the traditional employment relationship – reflected for example in a 'fair day's work for a fair day's pay' or an organisational career and a high level of job security – has broken down to be replaced by a much less certain set of arrangements. As a result, it is argued, the psychological contract of employees has been 'violated' by the organisation and its agents. Given what we know about the pace of change at work, this is a plausible analysis. However, our previous surveys have clearly shown that this is an exaggerated view of the impact of change. Most workers remain satisfied with their jobs, reasonably secure and committed, and willing to display high levels of motivation. They are sometimes comfortable with change; indeed they can welcome it and they are unlikely to report that there has been a serious violation of their psychological contract caused by organisational change or indeed by other experiences at work.

Despite these generally positive findings, there exists a substantial minority – ranging between one-fifth and one-third of workers depending on the issue – who are less content. These are often workers on the margins of employment, but they may also be found in certain sub-groups: for example, older workers feel less secure.

> 'One of the reasons for the growing interest in the concept of the psychological contract is a widespread belief that the traditional employment relationship ... has broken down to be replaced by a much less certain set of arrangements.'

Each year, the survey focuses on a particular theme that is explored in more depth. Previous years have covered motivation, fairness and change. This year we break new ground in covering two themes with a larger sample. The main theme is an exploration of the psychological contract in the public sector. The public sector has become distinctive as the main locus of trade union membership. At the same time, it retains a strong professional and service ethic. Both may make public sector workers less susceptible to corporate policy and practice. On the other hand, the public sector has experienced many years of change as successive governments try to manage it more effectively and in so doing have sometimes challenged aspects of the public sector ethos. So it is plausible to expect that a number of public sector workers will feel that their psychological contracts have been violated. There has been evidence in previous surveys of some differences between workers in the public and private sectors. It has not always been easy to determine how far any differences are due to the sector or due to the kind of people who choose to work in the public and private sectors. This year we should obtain a clearer picture. The 1998 Workplace Employment Relations Survey provided an opportunity to compare the two sectors. This revealed quite large differences on a number of issues covering both employment policy and practice as well as workers' reactions to these practices.[1] This will provide one point of comparison.

The second theme, which will play a more minor role, concerns what is commonly described as

work–life balance. In practice, of course, this is actually concerned with the balance between work and the rest of life. There has been a growing debate about the demands of work, reflected most obviously in the length of the working week and the pressure for policy to support family-friendly activities. Some of the questions that need further exploration include how far workers are willing accomplices in the lengthening of the working week, how much they value family-friendly policies and how much use they might make of family-friendly practices if they were available.

The survey has been analysed within a framework that has been used in previous years. This framework is presented in Figure 1. Within this, the state of the psychological contract is operationalised in terms of the extent to which workers believe that promises and commitments made to them by the organisation have been delivered, the level of fairness of treatment and the degree of trust in management to continue to deliver promises in the future. The rest of the framework outlines some of the potentially important influences on the psychological contract and the attitudes and behaviours that might be affected by a more or less positive psychological contract. All of these are covered in the survey. It should be noted that the survey explores *employee* views of the state of the psychological contract. It does not take account of the employer or organisational perspective. This would require a rather different study; however, the CIPD will soon be producing a report on this issue.[2]

---

1. The findings of the 1998 Workplace Employee Relations Survey can be found in CULLY M., O'REILLY A., WOODLAND S. and DIX G. *Britain at Work: As depicted by the 1998 Workplace Employee Relations Survey*. London, Routledge, 1999. An analysis that gives some prominence to comparisons between the results for the public and private sectors can be found in GUEST D., MICHIE J., SHEEHAN M. and CONWAY N. *Employment Relations, HRM and Business Performance*. London, Institute of Personnel and Development, 2000.

2. The report, based on a separate survey commissioned by the CIPD, will be published early in 2001.

The aims of the report

In summary, the aims of this report are to:

◻ assess the state of the employment relationship, and in particular the psychological contract, and note any changes from previous years and any trends over time

◻ identify the influences on, and consequences of, a more or less positive psychological contract

◻ explore in particular the state of the psychological contract among employees in the public sector

◻ compare responses across different parts of the public sector

◻ explore reactions to change in the public and private sectors

◻ examine perceptions of work–life balance and factors that determine whether an acceptable balance exists.

The structure of the report

The key findings are presented in the *Executive summary*. The main text of the report provides the full information on which these are based. Following this introductory chapter, a brief chapter outlines the sample and how it was obtained. Chapter 3 presents the descriptive findings concerning the influences on the psychological contract, such as human resource practices and the organisational climate. Chapter 4 then outlines the core results on the state of the psychological

Figure 1 | A model of the causes and consequences of the psychological contract

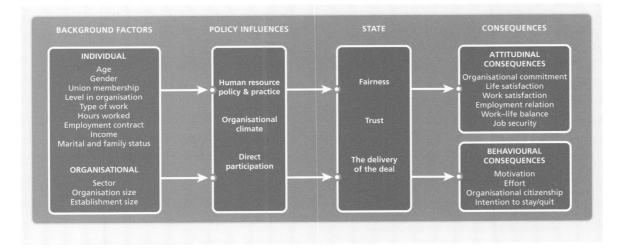

contract. Chapter 5 looks at attitudes that might be affected by the state of the psychological contract and Chapter 6 looks at behaviours such as level of motivation and planning to leave the organisation. Chapter 7 explores issues of work–life balance and general life satisfaction, while Chapter 8 reports the findings on the experience of change. Chapter 9 draws out any differences within the three main public sector groups. Chapter 10 highlights any changes over time in responses to core survey items and Chapter 11 provides some more general conclusions.

In each chapter we present the descriptive results. However, we also build a picture of the factors that influence these results. This is based on multivariate statistical analysis, but is presented in an easily digestible form. It helps to provide some insight into the 'why' as well as the 'what' of employee attitudes and behaviour and through this highlights policy implications.

2 | The survey process and the sample

◘ **The sample consisted of 500 workers from central government, 500 from local government, 500 from the health sector and 500 from private industry.**

◘ **The survey data were collected through telephone interviews.**

The sample

In previous years, a national sample of workers has been obtained through telephone interviews based on random digit-dialling. This is a well-established and well-researched approach to ensure a representative sample. However, this year it was decided to collect a larger sample from the public sector. The agreed target was 500 from central government, 500 from local government, 500 from the National Health Service and, as a basis for comparison, 500 from industry. The 500 from industry could be obtained using the normal process of random digit-dialling, but this was not feasible for the public sector groups.

The following procedure was used. First, the co-operation of the full range of government departments and agencies was sought and obtained. In most cases, their telephone directories were then used as a basis for random selection of staff for telephone interview. Where a department was reluctant to provide a directory, the department identified interviewees. Health sector trusts and local authorities were approached on a random basis and where co-operation was forthcoming, workers were selected, at random if possible, from telephone directories. In addition, Taylor Nelson Sofres conducts a regular programme of home-based interviews – a kind of omnibus survey – among a randomly selected sample of people in Britain. When interviews were conduced with those in the public sector, they were asked whether they would be willing to undergo a further telephone interview. Finally, a number of public sector employees were identified through the normal process of random digit-dialling.

There are a number of risks in this approach. Some people may be more willing to co-operate than others. For example, it is traditionally more difficult to find young single men at home for evening telephone interviews and some careful age and gender-based stratification of a national sample is therefore necessary. It may be that certain types of worker are easier to contact at work by telephone and some may be more willing to spend time being interviewed. However, it is unclear whether those co-operating are likely to be more or less satisfied. Furthermore, if there are built-in biases, they should be reasonably consistent at least across the three groups in the public sector. Therefore, while the process of sample selection was not ideal, it was difficult to see how it could be reasonably improved without incurring undue costs and delays.

In the event, the three public sector groups were formed from a combination of the three approaches to sample identification. It is clear that the health sector includes a number who work in private sector nursing homes and who are not therefore part of the public sector. We estimate that this is a maximum of 20 per cent of the health sector sample. It is probable that this process also resulted in slightly more people in administrative and management roles in the sample. However there was an attempt to ensure a range of type of job and grade within each part of the public sector. More rigorous controls to ensure a sample representative on age and gender were used in the selection of the private sector sample. We conducted some statistical analyses to determine whether those who were identified for the sample through different processes responded in different ways to the questions. There was some evidence that after controlling for sector, those who were identified through directories or the omnibus survey reported more scope for direct participation and more human resource practices. However, they did not differ on any of the attitude or behaviour items that are discussed in the following chapters, with one exception – they were more likely to engage in organisational citizenship behaviours. Since agreeing to participate in a survey could be construed as an indication of citizenship, this is not altogether surprising. While the absence of differences is encouraging, there is sufficient doubt about the randomness of the sample compared with previous years, to justify a note of caution about representativeness.

The interview content

The content of the survey is shaped by a number of factors. The first is that the interviews can only last for about 15 minutes. As a result, a single question may have to be asked where, in a longer interview or questionnaire, several questions on the same issue might provide a somewhat more reliable response. What this means is that some of the responses are indicative rather than conclusive. A second influence is the need to repeat at least some questions each year to identify any trends. A

third one is the need to ensure that questions are asked that cover the core model of the psychological contract, including its causes, state and consequences. Fourth, there need to be questions that provide sufficient background information about the sample. Finally, there needs to be scope to focus on the key topic that is being covered each year. In this case, it was work–life balance but additional attention also had to be given to the nature of work within the sectors.

There was an opportunity to provide an input to the content of the survey from public sector management and extensive discussions with the survey experts at Taylor Nelson Sofres and with the CIPD. The final control of the content remained with the research team.

The actual interviews were conducted mainly in July 2000. The timing may be significant since it followed closely on the Government's announcement of substantial funding for the National Health Service.

The workers in the survey

A full set of information about the sample is provided in the appendices. Below we list some of the key characteristics to provide a flavour of the workers whose responses are presented in some detail in the following chapters. All the indicators listed below form part of the background analysis in the chapters that follow. In other words, we are interested in whether any of these variables explain variations in response. Where they do so, this is indicated at the appropriate point and from this a picture gradually emerges of which organisational or individual factors explain differences in experiences, attitudes and behaviour at work:

- The total sample comprised 2,006 workers, including at least 500 from each sector.

- 80 per cent are full-time workers.

- 6 per cent have more than one job.

- 11 per cent work in locations with fewer than 10 workers, while 21 per cent work in establishments with more than 500 staff.

- 13 per cent work for organisations employing fewer than 100 people, while 60 per cent work for organisations employing more than 1,000.

- 23 per cent are in management jobs, 35 per cent in professional or semi-professional jobs, 29 per cent are in clerical and technical administration or sales and the remaining 13 per cent are in some sort of blue-collar job.

- 40 per cent consider themselves to be part of the management of the organisation, even if they are not always classified as being in management jobs.

- 20 per cent work in London.

- 6 per cent are employed on temporary contracts and 5 per cent on fixed-term contracts.

- 7 per cent work less than 20 hours a week and 50 per cent work more than 40 hours a week in practice.

- 93 per cent describe their ethnic background as white.

- 64 per cent are married, 25 per cent single and 10 per cent separated or divorced.

- 41 per cent have children of school age or younger.

- Average weekly pay before deductions ranges from less than £150 among 11 per cent to more than £500 among 17 per cent. 8 per cent refused to answer this question.

- 61 per cent of the sample is female.

- The sample contains 40 per cent who have at least a first degree and 10 per cent who have no formal qualifications.

- Age ranges from 21 per cent under 30 to 8 per cent over 55.

- 49 per cent belong to a trade union or recognised staff association.

3 | Determinants of the state of the psychological contract

◪ **The organisational climate in the public sector is considered more friendly, more bureaucratic but less dynamic than the private sector.**

◪ **Those working in central government report the highest number of human resource practices in place and those in industry report the lowest number.**

◪ **There is only modest scope for direct participation in day-to-day decisions about work – unless you are part of management, in which case there is plenty of scope.**

In this chapter we examine the background factors that can help to explain variations in the state of the psychological contract and in related attitudes and behaviour. In particular, we look, as in previous years, at the experience of human resource practices and at the scope for autonomy and decision-making in the job – what is sometimes described as direct participation. In previous surveys, both have been shown to have an important influence on the psychological contract. In addition, we introduce a simple measure of organisational climate.

Human resource practices

We asked all workers whether they had experienced certain practices or whether they knew that their employer had policies in place that applied to people like them. The list covers some of the core areas of human resource management, although it is geared as much to policies and practices that might affect employee well-being as to those expected to affect performance. A similar list has been used in the previous surveys, although the wording has been changed slightly this year on a number of items, making comparisons across the years a little risky.

The results are shown in Table 1. The figures in the table show the percentage in each of the four groups, and overall who reported that a particular practice or policy is in place. The figure at the bottom of the table shows the average number of practices out of the total of 11 reported by workers in each group. The responses indicate a widespread application of a number of the practices. For example, 91 per cent report that their organisation actively carries out equal opportunity practices, a response endorsed as strongly by women as by men. 81 per cent say their organisation takes active steps to prevent people like them being harassed or bullied at work. This figure calls into question claims that organisations are being slow to respond to issues of harassment and bullying at work. While there is a high positive response on practices associated with employee well-being, it is rather lower on the sort of practices sometimes associated with 'high-performance human resource management'. For example, only 38 per cent report a link between their pay and performance, and only 39 per cent participate in any kind of performance improvement and employee involvement teams.

Table 1 | Experience of human resource practices

	Central government	Local government	Health	Industry	Total
Your organisation actively carries out equal opportunity practices in the workplace	94	94	94	82	91
Your organisation takes active steps to prevent any kind of harassment or bullying for people like you	85	84	84	70	81
Your organisation keeps you well informed about business issues and how well it is doing	87	78	85	73	81
You have received some sort of training and development to update your skills in the past 12 months	89	81	84	68	80
You have received a formal appraisal during the past 12 months	89	61	58	57	66
There is a serious attempt to make the jobs of people like you as interesting and varied as possible	70	58	68	54	63
Your organisation offers some sort of family-friendly policies	77	52	63	34	57
Your organisation has a stated policy of deliberately avoiding compulsory redundancies and lay-offs	50	51	43	32	44
Your organisation usually tries to fill new positions in management from inside the organisation rather than recruiting externally	59	28	37	49	43
You have been personally involved in workplace decisions through, for example, self-directed work-teams, TQM, quality circles or involvement programmes during the past year	38	40	42	38	39
Your pay is related to your personal performance in some way through performance- or merit-related pay	85	15	15	37	38
Average number of practices	**8.23**	**6.42**	**6.71**	**5.94**	**6.83**

Note: All figures are expressed as percentages, with the exception of the final row.

There are statistically significant differences[1] between the four groups on all the practices except employee involvement, as well as differences on the overall number of practices that affect them. In general, those working in central government report the highest overall number of practices and the highest level of experience of each of the practices. At the other extreme, those working in industry in the private sector report the lowest overall number of practices and often the lowest uptake of each practice. There are exceptions to this. Performance-related pay is more common in industry than in the health sector or local government. So too is the tendency to fill management vacancies from within, although this item might be interpreted in slightly different ways in each sector. Employees in local government and the health sector tend to differ rather less. However, where significant differences between them do exist – on making jobs interesting, on filling management vacancies from within, on keeping people informed and on family-friendly polices – it is invariably employees in the health sector who are more likely to report that the practice is in place.

The evidence described in Table 1 suggests that there are differences between public and private sectors and within the public sector in the application of human resource management practices. Similar results were obtained in an analysis of the 1998 Workplace Employee Relations Survey, where the responses were provided by those responsible for the human resource practices. Furthermore, that survey also confirmed that the key differences lay in the greater adoption of practices associated with fairness of treatment and employee well-being rather than practices most likely to be associated with high performance. However, we can go a step further and explore other background factors that help to determine the number of human resource practices reported by staff in the different sectors. For this, we undertook a standard regression analysis, including the range of individual and organisational background factors listed in Chapter 2 that were common across the four groups of employees. Unfortunately, this means we had to omit specific job categories that applied to only a particular sector, such as nurse or social worker. These are considered in a later chapter. The main results are presented in Figure 2. This shows the beta weights, which provide some indication of the size of the association.[2]

1. Direct comparisons across the four groups are based on ANOVAS and statistically significant differences are reported at the .05 level or better.

2. All the results shown in Figure 2 and in subsequent figures are significant at the .0001 level or better unless otherwise indicated. Given the large sample size, it is possible for quite a large number of items to be statistically significant. We shall normally refer to other items that are significant at the .05 level or better in the text. The purpose of the figures is therefore to highlight the most important findings, taking more account of size effects.

Figure 2 | Determinants of the number of
human resource practices

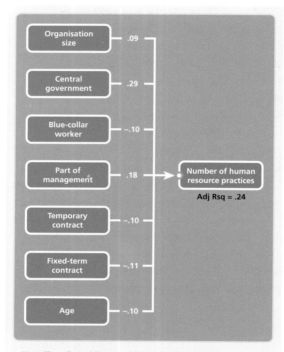

Note: The adjusted R-square (Adj Rsq) indicates the percentage
(when multiplied by 100) of variance explained in the outcome
by the 'predictor' variables. In the present case, for example, the
background variables explain 24 per cent of the variation in the
number of human resource practices.

The results in Figure 2 confirm that working in
central government is a major determinant of the
number of human resource practices experienced.
Those who see themselves as part of management
report that they experience more of the practices.
Conversely, blue-collar workers experience fewer
practices than those in senior management and
administration; so too do those on temporary and
fixed-term contracts and, perhaps more
surprisingly, those who are older. These, then, are
the key influences. Other still significant positive
influences, albeit displaying a slightly weaker
association, are working in the health sector,
having a higher income and being a trade union
member. Education level, perversely, is associated
with fewer reported practices. Together, these
background factors account for 24 per cent of the
variation in responses.

This set of results largely confirms what we know
from previous surveys. Those at senior levels with a
higher income in large organisations are the most
likely to experience 'progressive' human resource
practices. In contrast, lower-level, lower-income
and blue-collar workers are less likely to do so. In
other words, if these practices affect worker well-
being, then their impact is likely to be a function
of level in the organisation. Unions can help to
mitigate this effect. The key additional information
is that, even after these other background factors
have been taken into account, working in central
government and to a lesser extent in the health
sector still exerts an additional significant and
positive influence on the number of human
resource practices experienced.

'Those at senior levels with a higher income in large organisations are the most likely to experience "progressive" human resource practices.'

Scope for direct participation

Previous surveys have shown the importance of scope for direct participation for assessments of the state of the psychological contract. Workers value some control over decisions affecting their day-to-day work. Related research has also confirmed the importance of aspects of job design for a positive psychological contract. We therefore included a number of items, most of which have been used in previous surveys, to provide a measure of autonomy and control over day-to-day work decisions. We shall refer to this as direct participation.

We asked about the extent to which workers were able to take decisions concerning a range of work-related issues. Possible responses were 'most of the time' (scored 4), 'some of the time' (3), 'rarely'

(2) and 'never' (1). The responses are presented in Table 2, which shows the percentage who report that they can take the relevant type of decision 'most of the time'. This varies considerably, from 85 per cent who can carry out their work in the way they think best, to 14 per cent who can decide 'most of the time' where they work.

We undertook a factor analysis – a statistical process to determine whether the items were measuring some underlying construct – and found that all but two formed a single factor. The two, which we have excluded from subsequent analysis in the report, are shown at the bottom of Table 2. They are clearly of a different order to the rest. We therefore also omit them from the following analysis of direct participation. The other seven items were used to form a scale to measure the experience of direct participation.[3] When we look

Table 2 | Scope for direct participation

	Central government	Local government	Health	Industry	Total
MOST OF THE TIME:					
I carry out work in the way I think best	80	85	90	84	85
I plan my own work	69	63	62	47	61
I vary how I do my work	36	44	40	40	40
I can take time off work to deal with pressing non-work issues	40	29	27	31	32
I choose when I do my work	27	29	27	27	27
I choose the job assignments I work on	12	21	22	22	19
I choose where I do my work	11	15	14	17	14
I keep my work separate from the rest of my life	65	56	59	63	61
I talk to my immediate boss about problems I have outside work	11	17	16	19	16
Average response (first seven items only)	2.88	2.82	2.76	2.65	2.78

Note: All figures are expressed as percentages, with the exception of the final row.

3. The alpha score for these seven items is .71.

at the average score, which is shown at the bottom of each column in Table 2, we can see that the typical response of 2.78 indicates that on average workers can take decisions about their own work rather less often than 'some of the time' (a score of 3) but more often than 'rarely' (a score of 2). Once again those working in central government report the highest average score, closely followed by local government workers, with private industry workers lagging behind. Given the nature of the work in the public sector and issues of professional autonomy, we should not be surprised by these findings. The private sector responses are significantly lower than those for both central and local government employees. More surprisingly, the health sector responses are also significantly lower than those in central government.

We can again conduct a fuller analysis to determine whether the sector differences remain when we take into account other organisational and individual background factors. The results of

the regression analysis are shown in Figure 3. Once again, only the highly significant results are shown.

The results in Figure 3 generally conform to common-sense expectations. Those with most scope to make decisions about their day-to-day work are part of management and have a higher income and higher level of education, which together imply that they are more senior and/or in positions to exercise professional autonomy. Conversely, blue-collar workers report less autonomy. So too do trade union members. Still statistically significant but at a slightly lower level, the results show that those in local government (but not, in this case, those in central government) are more likely to report direct participation than those in private industry, while those in large establishments and those in white-collar clerical jobs are less likely to experience scope for direct participation at work. These background factors explain 22 per cent of the variation in responses and suggest that organisational level is rather more important than sector in explaining variations in scope for direct participation. However, even after taking into account these other background influences, local government employees still report higher levels of direct participation than private industry employees.

Organisational climate

In a short interview, it is almost impossible to gain any serious insight into organisational culture. Conventional measures of climate also tend to include large numbers of questions. We therefore adopted a different approach, asking interviewees to respond to a number of words and indicate whether or not they described their organisation. The precise question was 'How would you describe the cultural climate of your organisation? Would you say it was … ?' This was followed by the 11

Figure 3 | Determinants of direct participation

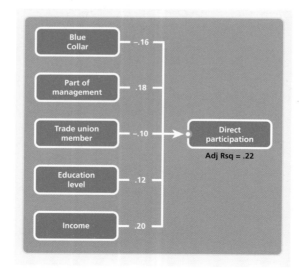

items shown in Table 3 to which an answer of yes or no was required. Statistical analysis showed that these words fell into three distinct groups reflecting 'friendliness', 'dynamic' and 'bureaucratic' features of the organisation.[4]

The results with respect to the 'friendliness' dimension are very positive. Most people describe their organisation as *ethical, friendly, fair-minded, public-spirited* and *supportive*. Only *'trusting'* gets a markedly lower response, more particularly among central government employees. More generally, those working in private industry give a lower response. Upon closer examination this can be attributed largely to lower responses on the *'public-spirited'* and *'ethical'* items. Statistical comparisons reveal that the health sector and local government score significantly higher than central government and private industry across the set of items on 'friendliness'.

The results for the 'dynamic' dimension are much less positive, with low scores on the *dynamic* and *creative* items. Scores on *forward-looking* are much higher, perhaps indicating optimism about the future. Central government employees give significantly lower scores than those in private industry and the health sector.

Table 3 | Perceptions of the organisational climate

		Central government	Local government	Health	Industry	Total
FRIENDLINESS						
% agreeing climate is :	Ethical	94	93	96	83	92
	Friendly	90	90	93	88	90
	Public-spirited	89	91	88	73	85
	Fair-minded	83	82	82	81	82
	Supportive	82	83	85	77	82
	Trusting	60	72	71	71	69
DYNAMIC						
% agreeing climate is :	Forward-looking	82	79	85	79	81
	Creative	43	55	51	60	52
	Dynamic	33	36	47	46	41
BUREAUCRATIC						
% agreeing climate is :	Bureaucratic	74	73	65	53	66
	Constraining	63	55	57	47	56

4. We conducted a factor analysis of these items. Technically, it is not good practice to factor-analyse dichotomous yes/no responses, but it can give an initial indication of groupings and in this case the three factors emerged quite clearly. We could then turn them into scales and they had alphas of .77 for friendliness, .62 for dynamic and .37 for bureaucratic. This last alpha score is well below the acceptable level, so this variable was excluded from subsequent analysis. In practice, because of the high number of positive responses, more particularly on the first factor, we took a count of the number of workers in each group who had said 'yes' to all the items in the factor. This created three dichotomous variables (eg 'yes' on all friendliness items or not), two of which, friendliness and dynamic, are used in subsequent analyses.

> ' ... these results provide an initial indication that central government employees may not be as positive about their organisational climate as those in other sectors.'

The final factor contains two items concerned with bureaucracy. Perhaps predictably, employees in central government report significantly higher scores than other sectors, while those in private industry report scores that are significantly lower.

Taken as a whole, these results provide an initial indication that central government employees may not be as positive about their organisational climate as those in other sectors. We can use the regression analysis where we take account of other factors to determine how robust this finding is. The results of the analysis of all the background influences on the 'friendliness' dimension of organisational climate are shown in Figure 4.

The results in Figure 4 confirm that after taking account of other background factors, employees in both the health sector and local government report a more friendly organisational climate than those in private industry. The only other highly significant background influence is trade union membership, which is associated with more negative perceptions of the organisational climate. Two other background items are statistically

significant, albeit at a lower level; those with more educational qualifications and those working longer hours report a less friendly climate. While these findings are of interest, we should note that background factors account for only 3 per cent of the variation in responses, leaving a lot of the differences in responses unexplained.

The background influences on the 'dynamic' dimension are shown in Figure 5. The results confirm that workers in central government and also local government are particularly likely to believe their organisation lacks dynamism. Those who consider themselves to be part of management are more likely to describe their organisation as dynamic, perhaps because they share some of the responsibility for change. Two other background factors are statistically significant at a lower level. Older workers are less likely to view their organisation as dynamic, while those from ethnic minorities are more likely to do so. Once again the level of variation in responses explained by the background factors is low, only 4 per cent, so the results should be treated with caution.

Figure 4 | Determinants of a 'friendly' climate

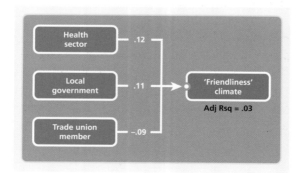

Figure 5 | Determinants of a 'dynamic' climate

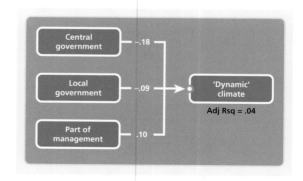

> **'The analysis has also revealed that there is more scope for direct participation in day-to-day decisions about work in the public sector ... .'**

The final analysis in this section concerns the 'bureaucratic' dimension. The results are shown in Figure 6 below. The results are straightforward and reflect popular prejudices. Those working in larger organisations and in the public sector as opposed to the private sector believe that their organisation is more bureaucratic. No other background factors have any marked influence. However, it should be noted that only a small amount of the variation in responses is accounted for with the factors that were included in the analysis.

Summary

We have now completed the analysis of the background factors that are susceptible to management policy and practice. The analysis confirms that the public sector in general and central government in particular is more likely to have adopted a number of human resource practices of the sort typically designed to promote fairness of treatment and employee well-being. This finding is in line with other evidence and contradicts a view that private industry is more progressive and dynamic in its application of

human resource practices. Of course, this leaves unanswered any questions about the effectiveness with which these practices are deployed, an issue that may be partly answered in the next section on the state of the psychological contract.

The analysis has also revealed that there is more scope for direct participation in day-to-day decisions about work in the public sector in general, and in central and local government in particular. However, level in the organisation is probably an even more important influence. Finally, we explored aspects of organisational climate. Three separate factors emerged, which we labelled *friendliness, dynamic* and *bureaucratic*. The public sector scored more strongly than the private sector on friendliness and bureaucratic and less strongly on dynamism. Closer inspection revealed that friendliness was more likely in the health and local government sectors and that central government, followed by local government, was particularly likely to be perceived as lacking in dynamism. However, while we can be quite confident that we are explaining reasonable levels of influence on variations in human resource practices and direct participation, the background factors explain only small amounts of the variation in organisational climate.

In the next chapter, we shall explore how far the policies and practices as well as the organisational climate help to explain variations in the state of the psychological contract. Since the bureaucratic dimension of organisational climate did not prove to be a sufficiently robust measure, it is excluded from the subsequent analysis.

Figure 6 | Determinants of a 'bureaucratic' climate

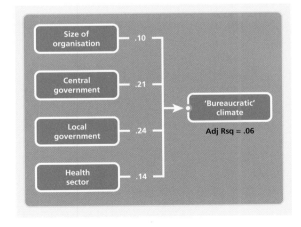

4 | The state of the psychological contract

◩ **Two in every five workers do not believe they have a fair balance between their effort and their rewards.**

◩ **49 per cent trust their immediate manager to look after their best interests, but only 25 per cent trust senior management to do so.**

◩ **More human resource practices, more direct participation and a friendly, dynamic organisational climate are all associated with a better psychological contract. Despite this, central government workers are particularly likely to report a poor psychological contract.**

The psychological contract is concerned with the fulfilment of perceived promises and obligations. The *state* of the psychological contract, which forms the core of the analysis in this chapter, is operationalised as perceptions of the extent to which promises have been met, the fairness of treatment associated with promises and trust that management will look after a worker's best interests and continue to do so. In short, it is about delivery of promises, fairness and trust that, arguably, lie at the heart of the employment relationship. As noted in Chapter 1, in this study we explore the state of the psychological contract only from the perspective of employees. However, this inevitably provides insights for employers concerning reactions to their policies and practices. In this chapter, we start by examining the promises that workers' believe the organisation has made to them, then we look at how far they have kept these promises. The next step is to explore fairness and trust. Finally, we explore the determinants of the state of the psychological contract and look for any variations between sectors.

Promises and commitments

All interviewees were asked whether they believed their organisation had made promises or commitments to them on a range of issues. This leaves unstated whether these promises are explicit or implicit, public or private, general or specific to the individual and who made them on behalf of the organisation. For our present purposes, the important point is whether or not a worker believes that the promise or commitment has been made. The list covers some of the core items identified in previous surveys, including both specific outcomes and certain processes or ways of managing. The results are presented in Table 4. This shows whether or not a promise is believed to have been made; then it shows part of the response concerning whether or not it has been kept. Four responses were possible, from 'fully kept' through 'largely kept' and 'partly kept' to 'not kept at all'. The table shows the percentage of those who believed promises had been made who said they had been fully kept or not kept at all. It also shows the average response for the group across the range from fully kept (4) to not kept at all (1).

The responses show that a large majority of workers believe promises have been made about key processes, such as ensuring equal opportunity and equality of treatment. Only in central government does this extend, for a majority of workers, to help with problems outside work. Over two-thirds believe they have received some sort of

Table 4 | Promises made and kept by the organisation

WHETHER THE ORGANISATION HAS PROMISED OR COMMITTED ITSELF TO:	Central government	Local government	Health	Industry	Total
provide you with a reasonably secure job					
promise made	71	70	75	68	71
promise fully kept	66	59	69	64	65
promise not kept	1	0	0	1	0
provide you with fair pay for the work you do					
promise made	65	71	70	71	69
promise fully kept	34	54	53	52	49
promise not kept	10	2	4	3	5
provide you with a career					
promise made	69	49	54	47	55
promise fully kept	32	51	57	48	46
promise not kept	7	1	2	5	4
provide you with interesting work					
promise made	49	44	48	42	46
promise fully kept	33	47	50	49	45
promise not kept	2	0	1	0	1
ensure fair treatment by managers and supervisors					
promise made	93	88	85	76	85
promise fully kept	37	45	52	45	45
promise not kept	2	2	2	4	2
ensure equality of treatment					
promise made	90	91	86	77	86
promise fully kept	46	50	58	51	51
promise not kept	3	1	1	2	2
help you deal with problems you encounter outside work					
promise made	51	37	39	31	39
promise fully kept	33	39	41	43	38
promise not kept	2	1	1	2	1
Average across items[1]	3.10	3.26	3.36	3.21	3.23

Note: All figures are expressed as percentages, with the exception of the final row.

1. Four-point scale ranging from 'fully kept' (4) to 'not kept at all' (1).

> **' ... significantly more promises are believed to have been made in central government than elsewhere and significantly fewer in private industry than in any part of the public sector.'**

promise about job security and about fair pay. Rather fewer believe they have received promises about a career or interesting work. A comparison across sectors reveals that significantly more promises are believed to have been made in central government than elsewhere and significantly fewer in private industry than in any part of the public sector. The number of promises appears to be quite closely linked to the number of human resource practices in place. This possibility can be explored more fully by analysing the background factors that explain variations in the number of promises made. The results are shown in Figure 7.

The results show that working in central government is not in itself the key factor influencing the number of promises made. Instead, the key factors associated with the number of promises made are all policy-related and to some extent under management control. The most important is the number of human resource practices in place. This is not surprising since many of these practices imply promises. It is also worth noting that more of these are in place in central government than elsewhere. The other policy-related background factors are the extent to which the climate is perceived as friendly and the scope for direct participation. Other still significant but slightly less important influences are trade union membership, which is associated with more promises, and age, educational level and being on a temporary contract, which are all associated with fewer promises.

Have promises been kept?

A key component of the state of the psychological contract is the extent to which promises have been kept. The results are contained in Table 4. The pattern of results suggests that, on the whole, promises are not believed to have been fully kept. At the same time, total violation to the extent that promises have not been kept at all is rare. To be more specific, for the whole sample, 65 per cent believe that promises with respect to job security have been fully kept and 51 per cent believe this also applies to ensuring equality of treatment. At the other extreme, only 38 per cent believe that commitments to help with problems arising outside work have been fully kept. Very small numbers say promises have not been kept at all, ranging from 5 per cent with respect to fair pay to 0 per cent for job security. Rather more admit that some promises have been only partly kept. However, a look at the average responses on the range from 1 to 4 shows that typical scores are above 3, suggesting that promises have been fully or largely kept.

Figure 7 I Determinants of number of promises made

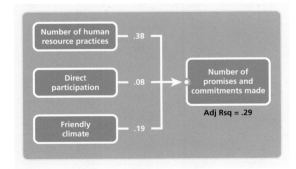

Looking across sectors, some clear differences emerge. Central government, where workers reported the largest number of promises, also has the most that have not been fully kept. This is particularly notable with respect to fair pay for work done, the promise of a career and the provision of interesting work. More generally, with the exception of promises regarding job security, workers in central government report fewer promises fully kept. Factor analysis confirmed that six of the seven promises could be combined into a single factor (the exception is the item on fair pay, which fits better with other items on fair pay) and we can make comparisons on scores on the single factor of promises delivered.[2] This shows, once again, that workers in central government report significantly fewer promises kept than workers in the health and local government sectors. Central government is lower but not significantly lower

than private industry. Health sector workers are more likely to report promises kept than private industry workers. In summary, central government employees report the most promises made and the smallest proportion kept.

Fairness

In previous surveys we have explored issues of fairness in some detail. For this survey, we retained two core items, which are shown in Table 5.

The results in Table 5 reveal a widespread sense of unfairness with respect to the effort–reward bargain in general and fair pay in particular. It is strongest among employees in central government, although dissatisfaction with the fairness of pay is also strongly felt in the health sector.

Table 5 | Fairness

	Central government	Local government	Health	Industry	Total
OVERALL, DO YOU FEEL YOU ARE FAIRLY REWARDED FOR THE AMOUNT OF EFFORT YOU PUT INTO YOUR JOB?					
yes – definitely	21	28	30	32	28
yes – probably	35	36	35	37	36
no – probably not	23	20	18	15	19
no – definitely not	21	15	16	15	17
DO YOU FEEL YOU ARE FAIRLY PAID FOR THE WORK YOU DO?					
yes – definitely	18	31	25	35	27
yes – probably	31	28	30	32	30
no – probably not	23	24	17	14	19
no – definitely not	28	17	29	19	23

Note: All figures are expressed as percentages.

2. The alpha scores for the six-item measure of delivery of promises or commitments is .74. For the three fairness items it is .75 and for the three trust items .79. When they are combined into a single measure of the state of the psychological contract, the alpha score is .86.

A comparison across sectors on the combined measure of fairness, which includes the item on delivery of promises about pay, shows significant differences, with central government employees reporting lower levels of fairness than all other groups. At the other end of the range, private industry employees report higher levels of fairness than those in central government and the health sector. Local government employees fall somewhere in the middle between private industry and health sector employees. On this basis, it appears that with respect to fairness of treatment, which in practice means fairness of the effort–reward bargain, private sector employees report better treatment than their public sector counterparts. However, this hides considerable

variation within the public sector. More generally, it should be noted that across the board, levels of fairness are rather low, with about two out of five employees reporting that they do not feel fairly treated with respect to the effort–reward arrangements.

Trust

Trust is the final component of the measure of the state of the psychological contract. Whereas fairness and delivery of promises reflect past or current behaviour, trust is more oriented towards expectations of future treatment. It was covered in the survey by three items, which are shown in Table 6.

Table 6 | Trust in management and the organisation

	Central government	Local government	Health	Industry	Total
TO WHAT EXTENT DO YOU TRUST YOUR IMMEDIATE MANAGER TO LOOK AFTER YOUR BEST INTERESTS?					
a lot	48	49	52	47	49
somewhat	33	28	28	26	29
only a little	12	13	11	14	13
not at all	6	7	7	11	8
TO WHAT EXTENT DO YOU TRUST SENIOR MANAGEMENT TO LOOK AFTER YOUR BEST INTERESTS?					
a lot	14	26	28	31	25
somewhat	40	37	36	29	35
only a little	27	22	20	18	22
not at all	18	13	14	18	16
IN GENERAL, HOW MUCH DO YOU TRUST THE ORGANISATION TO KEEP ITS PROMISES OR COMMITMENTS TO YOU AND OTHER EMPLOYEES?					
a lot	24	32	30	35	30
somewhat	49	44	45	39	44
only a little	18	17	17	15	17
not at all	8	7	7	10	8

Note: All figures are expressed as percentages.

'There are higher levels of trust in the immediate manager than in senior management. ... there is also higher trust in the potentially abstract entity of the organisation than in senior management.'

The results in Table 6 show cautious levels of trust with interesting variations across the three items. There are higher levels of trust in the immediate manager than in senior management. However, contrary to expectation, there is also higher trust in the potentially abstract entity of the organisation than in senior management. This may also be a function of the specific focus of the question. The results also suggest sector differences, with central government employees appearing to display less trust in both senior management and the organisation as a whole. However, this is not confirmed in the more detailed statistical analysis, where the results just fail to reach significance.

Figure 8 | Determinants of the psychological contract

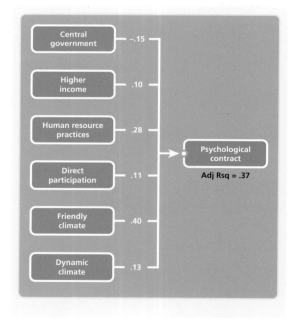

Explaining variations in the state of the psychological contract

The items measuring perceptions of delivery of promises or commitments, fairness and trust can be combined into a single measure of the overall state of the psychological contract. As we have already seen, there are quite marked variations in responses on each of the three sets of items. We now turn to an examination of the background and policy factors that help to explain why some workers report a generally positive psychological contract while for others the picture is much less encouraging. The analysis is again based on the use of regressions and the results are shown in Figure 8.

The results in Figure 8 confirm a pattern of results that has appeared in previous surveys. The various background and policy factors account for 37 per cent of the variation in responses on the combined measure of the psychological contract. The number of human resource practices and the scope for direct participation are both powerful explanatory factors. Income level has also appeared in previous surveys. This year there are two additional sets of items. The first is the measure of organisational climate, with those reporting a friendlier and more dynamic climate also reporting a better psychological contract. The final highly significant factor is the experience of working in central government, which has a negative influence on the state of the psychological contract. This is a particularly powerful factor because those in central government also reported the highest number of human resource practices and high levels of direct participation. Despite these 'advantages', which in themselves have a positive influence, central government employees are more likely to report fewer promises kept, lower fairness and less trust.

> ' ... both the number of human resource practices and the scope for direct participation are strongly associated with a better psychological contract.'

A number of other background factors also exert a significant association with the state of the psychological contract, albeit slightly less strong than the items in Figure 8. The only additional item that has a positive influence is being a blue-collar as opposed to a management-level worker. The other associations are negative. Therefore, those who work longer hours, trade union members, those working in larger organisations and those from ethnic minorities are all likely to report a poorer psychological contract. It is perhaps worth noting at this point that trade union membership appears to be associated with a range of more negative responses; since this seems to transcend occupational level, there may be something about being a union member that influences responses. Evidence from previous surveys strongly suggests that this cannot be explained by workers joining unions because they are dissatisfied.

Summary

The results in this chapter confirm that the model of the causes and consequences of the psychological contract presented in Chapter 1 receives strong support. It is important to emphasise that this is a cross-sectional survey and we cannot therefore assert cause and effect. However, evidence from the longitudinal analysis conducted in 1999[3] supports the causal links hypothesised in the model. In the present survey, both the number of human resource practices and the scope for direct participation are strongly associated with a better psychological contract. It is, of course, possible that all these responses reflect the problems of a self-report survey with internal consistency and high inter-correlation of items. The correlation table shown in Appendix 3 suggests that this cannot offer more than a very small proportion of the explanation.

The second key finding is that central government employees are particularly likely to report a poorer psychological contract. Since they also had greater experience of human resource practices and of direct participation, this is a strong finding. The descriptive results presented above confirm that the responses are spread across fulfilment of promises, fairness and trust. Since their responses differ from those in the local government and health sector, the causes appear to lie beyond a simple public sector phenomenon. We shall return to this issue in a later chapter when we look more closely at differences within each sector. For the present, we might speculate that the human resource practices and job autonomy are reflections of a pattern of expectations about work that are not being met at present. By implication, some process of over-promising or of breach of expectations has occurred.

3. The CIPD report *Organisational Change and the Psychological Contract* will be published late in 2000.

5 | Attitudes to work

◪ **More than 80 per cent of workers are either moderately or highly satisfied with their work.**

◪ **Most workers feel quite a lot of loyalty to their organisation, but many feel it is not reciprocated by the organisation.**

◪ **Very few workers are worried about their job security.**

In this chapter we explore responses to a range of conventional attitude questions. These cover work satisfaction, commitment to the organisation, job security and perceptions of worker–management employment relations. All of these have been used in previous surveys in this series, and in these surveys all have been closely associated with the state of the psychological contract.

Work satisfaction

Satisfaction with work was explored through a single item. Ideally we would have asked more questions; however, it has been established for job satisfaction that a single global question covers much of the variation that is picked up in a fuller set of questions, so it provides a reasonable indicator of general satisfaction with work. The question asked for satisfaction with work on a 10-point scale, from totally satisfied to totally dissatisfied. We have combined the responses into three categories: low (1–3), medium (4–7), and high (8–10) satisfaction. The results for the main groups are shown in Table 7.

Comparisons across the four groups reveal some statistically significant differences, with health sector workers more satisfied than all the other groups and local government workers also more satisfied than those in central government. Indeed, central government workers are the least satisfied overall.

We conducted a regression analysis to determine whether these differences remained after other background factors had been taken into account. The background variables account for 32 per cent of the variation in responses. The results for this

Table 7 | Work satisfaction

	Central government	Local government	Health	Industry	Total
high satisfaction	38	44	50	46	43
medium satisfaction	55	46	43	41	47
low satisfaction	7	9	8	12	9
average score	6.43	6.76	7.04	6.68	6.73

Note: All figures are expressed as percentages, with the exception of the final row.

' ... levels of general satisfaction with work remain reasonably high, although there is some evidence of decline over the years.'

are shown in Figure 9. This confirms that after controlling for all other factors, health sector workers are more satisfied with their work. It also confirms the importance of a friendly and dynamic climate. It draws attention to lower satisfaction among those with higher educational qualifications. However, above all it reinforces the importance of a positive psychological contract.

In addition to these highly significant associations, a number of other background factors also exert some influence on work satisfaction. Those reporting more scope for direct participation are more satisfied. So too are older workers and blue-collar workers when compared with those in management. Set against these associations, men are less likely to be satisfied.

In summary, levels of general satisfaction with work remain reasonably high, with little evidence of change over the years. Health sector workers report the highest level of satisfaction. Central government employees appear to be least satisfied

with their work. Although they do not emerge so clearly when other factors are taken into account, it should be borne in mind that they reported a poorer psychological contract, and the state of the psychological contract is the item that has the strongest association with work satisfaction.

Organisational commitment

While work satisfaction is normally linked to the job and the immediate circumstances surrounding it, commitment to the organisation is a broader measure of attachment to the organisation, typically reflected in identification with the goals and values of the organisation, a willingness to do things for the organisation and a desire to belong to and stay with the organisation. This implies that high levels of commitment might be associated with higher performance and lower labour turnover. In practice it has shown only weak links to performance but consistent links to labour retention. In a tight labour market it can therefore be an important indicator.

Figure 9 | Determinants of work satisfaction

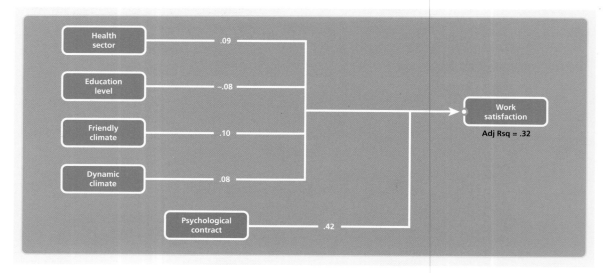

In this survey, organisational commitment was measured through two items, which emphasised the loyalty and identification aspects. For the first time we also added an item asking how much loyalty the organisation shows in return. For convenience and comparison, it is also shown in Table 8.

An initial point to note in these responses is the widespread perception that the level of loyalty workers report to their organisation is not reciprocated. In general, workers felt that the organisation shows lower levels of loyalty in return. Overall, while only 12 per cent of workers believe they show little or no loyalty to their

organisation, 27 per cent believe their organisation shows little or no loyalty to them. We have no way of knowing whether these are accurate perceptions, but they reflect either a low level of reciprocal commitment or a failure on the part of the organisation to provide effective feedback and communication.

The second point to emphasise is that commitment to the organisation is significantly higher among workers in the health sector than in all other groups. It is higher in local government than in central government. In other words, the pattern of results is similar to that found for work satisfaction and shows that commitment is lowest

Table 8 | Organisational commitment

	Central government	Local government	Health	Industry	Total
HOW MUCH LOYALTY WOULD YOU SAY YOU FEEL TOWARDS THE ORGANISATION YOU WORK FOR AS A WHOLE?					
a lot of loyalty	42	53	59	50	51
some loyalty	43	35	32	35	37
only a little loyalty	10	8	6	9	8
no loyalty at all	5	3	3	5	4
HOW PROUD ARE YOU TO TELL PEOPLE WHO YOU WORK FOR?					
very proud indeed	19	26	37	31	28
quite proud	44	44	42	36	41
not very proud	21	19	12	16	17
not at all proud	15	11	7	15	12
don't know	1	1	1	1	1
HOW MUCH LOYALTY DO YOU FEEL THE ORGANISATION SHOWS TOWARDS YOU?					
a lot of loyalty	19	28	32	31	27
some loyalty	52	45	42	38	44
only a little loyalty	20	20	17	19	19
no loyalty at all	8	7	7	11	8
don't know	1	1	1	1	

Note: All figures are expressed as percentages.

' ... levels of commitment to the organisation are largely influenced by the policies and practices of the organisation.'

among those working in central government. We checked this more carefully through the regression analysis where we control for other background factors.[1] The results are shown in Figure 10.

The more rigorous analysis summarised in Figure 10 confirms that health sector workers are more committed and central government workers less committed than others. The analysis also confirms the continuing importance of human resource practices and of a positive organisational climate and the considerable impact of a positive psychological contract. Ethnic minority workers also display higher levels of commitment to their organisation. In addition to these highly significant results, a number of other factors also exert a significant influence. Those who report high levels of direct participation and those who work long

hours are likely to be more committed. Older workers are also likely to report higher levels of commitment. In contrast, those who are single and those who have higher educational qualifications report lower levels of commitment.

In summary, levels of commitment to the organisation are influenced by the policies and practices of the organisation. Where these are perceived by workers to provide a more friendly and dynamic environment, where high numbers of human resource practices are in place and work autonomy is permitted and where the promises inherent in the human resource practices are kept, reflected in a positive psychological contract, then commitment to the organisation is significantly higher. This is more likely in the health sector and least likely in central government.

Figure 10 | Determinants of organisational commitment

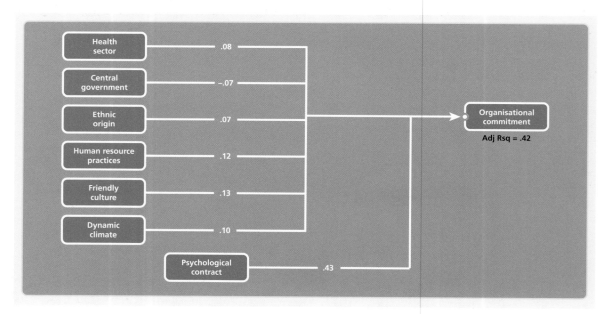

Job security

There has been much debate about levels of job security among the British workforce. Objective indicators reveal that many people still remain with the same employer for a number of years, but at the other extreme there is a minority who experience considerable churn. This is an issue on which it might be reasonable to expect differences between the public sector, where jobs have traditionally been more secure, and the private sector, where change has been more marked. At the same time, we need to draw a distinction between objective indicators of job security, such as tenure, and subjective indicators that reflect the level of individual anxiety about future employment. Indeed, previous surveys in this series have shown that older workers who have long tenure and have never experienced job loss are among those who feel the least secure.

This year we used a single item to tap job security. In previous surveys we have sometimes asked a number of questions and this is the most representative. The results are shown in Table 9.

The responses confirm that job security is generally high across workers in all sectors. While the largest proportion indicate that they feel 'fairly' secure, only a small proportion report feelings of insecurity. On the basis of a straight comparison, central government workers appear to be the most secure and are significantly more secure than those in private industry and in local government. Health sector workers are also more secure than those in private industry.

These differences remain when we take account of other background factors. The relevant results are shown in Figure 11 and the background factors account for 21 per cent of the variation in responses. This confirms that workers in the health sector and more particularly in central government report higher levels of job security than those in private industry. Job security is also associated with a better psychological contract. Predictably, job security is much lower among those on temporary and fixed-term contracts. The only other factors that are significantly associated with job security are age, with older workers once again feeling less secure, and a friendly climate, which is associated with greater job security.

Table 9 | Job security

	Central government	Local government	Health	Industry	Total
HOW DO YOU FEEL ABOUT YOUR PRESENT JOB SECURITY?					
very secure	45	35	41	31	38
fairly secure	45	50	50	49	48
fairly insecure	6	9	6	13	8
very insecure	3	5	4	6	5

Note: All figures are expressed as percentages.

Employment relations

Employment relations lie at the heart of this annual survey. We explore general perceptions of employment relations through a single item, which asks for a global assessment. The results are shown in Table 10.

On this item, there are no significant differences between the four groups. All broadly agree that in general relations between employees and management are good or at least fair. Workers in industry tend to be slightly more extreme, with a larger number saying relations are either 'excellent' or 'very poor'.

Figure 11 | Determinants of job security

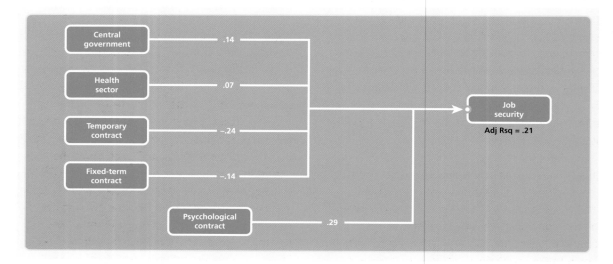

Table 10 | Employment relations

	Central government	Local government	Health	Industry	Total
OVERALL, HOW WOULD YOU RATE RELATIONS BETWEEN EMPLOYEES AND MANAGEMENT AT YOUR ORGANISATION?					
excellent	5	10	10	15	10
good	47	49	50	47	48
fair	39	28	29	23	30
poor	7	9	8	9	8
very poor	2	3	2	5	3

Note: All figures are expressed as percentages.

'... organisation policy and practice, reflected in climate, human resource management and the psychological contract, have a key bearing on assessments of the general state of employment relations.'

We conducted the usual regression analysis to determine what background and policy factors influenced variations in perceptions. The results for the highly significant items are shown in Figure 12.

The results in Figure 12 confirm the typical pattern from previous analyses, with favourable assessments of employment relations being positively associated with more human resource practices, a more friendly and dynamic climate and above all a positive assessment of the state of the psychological contract. In addition, a few other factors had a significant influence. In larger organisations, assessments were more negative. Workers on temporary and fixed-term contracts were likely to offer a more positive assessment of employment relations, possibly because they were less centrally involved.

In summary, organisation policy and practice, reflected in climate, human resource management and the psychological contract, have a key bearing on assessments of the general state of employment relations. It is worth noting that trade union membership does not have a significant influence on this item, despite earlier evidence that trade union members tend to be more critical and less positive in their assessments of a number of aspects of policy and practice.

Summary

We have now covered the items that reflect employee attitudes. They confirm the broad model of the psychological contract in showing that in each case the most important influence on responses is the state of the psychological contract. However, other background factors such as organisational climate, human resource practices and scope for direct participation, all of which helped to shape the state of the psychological contract, continue to exert a direct influence as well as an indirect influence through the psychological contract. This confirms the importance of these issues, all of which are a consequence of management policy, practice and general behaviour. The results also confirm the more positive attitudes among workers in the health sector and the tendency for those working in central government to be less positive.

Figure 12 | Determinants of employment relations

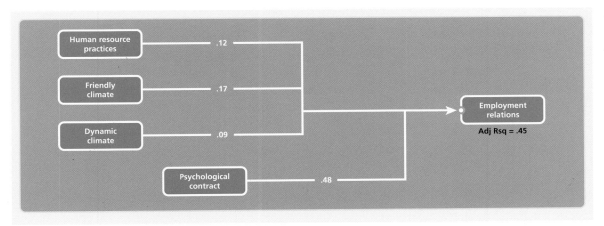

6 | Employee behaviour

◧ **More than half of the workers surveyed say that when they get up in the morning they look forward to going to work most or all of the time.**

◧ **25 per cent say they are working flat out and could not imagine working any harder. A further 43 per cent say they are working 'very hard'.**

◧ **58 per cent feel a strong obligation to go to work, even if they do not feel particularly well.**

◧ **Almost twice as many people working in private industry as in the public sector say they are likely to leave their organisation in the next year.**

In this chapter we describe the results for a number of employee behaviours. These concern motivation, effort, organisational citizenship behaviour and intention to leave the organisation. In the past we have tried to obtain self-ratings of performance but these have not proved to be very satisfactory, so we did not repeat the questions this year. The model assumes that attitudes influence behaviour. In other words, a more committed worker will be less likely to want to leave and a more satisfied worker will be more motivated. As already noted, we must be duly cautious in making any claims about cause and effect, but we can explore interesting associations and these are reported in the present chapter along with the descriptive results.

Motivation

In one of the previous surveys in this sequence, we explored motivation in some detail. One of the key findings was a clear distinction between what we now term motivation, which is essentially intrinsic and is something that comes from a worker, and effort, which is largely driven by extrinsic factors such as workload and the demands of the public,

the boss or even the work-team. We therefore treat the two concepts separately, using the items that most centrally reflect the concepts as identified in that earlier survey.

Motivation was measured with the two items shown in Table 11.

The responses reveal generally high levels of motivation. There is a minority – some 14–18 per cent, found more in central government and private industry – who report low motivation. This is confirmed by a statistical comparison across the four sub-samples. The two items can be combined for the purposes of further analysis.[1] The results then confirm that workers in the health and local government sectors report significantly higher motivation than those in central government and the private sector.

Once again we can take this a step further with the more rigorous regression analysis exploring the influence of the range of background factors. This time, the attitudinal responses have been added in. The results are shown in Figure 13, which includes only the highly significant results.

1. alpha .70.

Table 11 | Motivation at work

	Central government	Local government	Health	Industry	Total
HOW MOTIVATED DO YOU FEEL IN YOUR PRESENT JOB?					
very motivated	33	39	44	34	38
fairly motivated	50	48	48	47	48
not very motivated	15	9	5	13	10
not at all motivated	3	4	3	5	4
WHEN YOU GET UP IN THE MORNING, HOW OFTEN DO YOU REALLY LOOK FORWARD TO GOING TO WORK?					
all the time	7	11	12	11	10
most of the time	36	49	55	37	45
sometimes	34	26	20	29	27
rarely	15	9	7	11	11
never	8	4	5	11	7

Note: All figures are expressed as percentages.

Figure 13 | Determinants of motivation

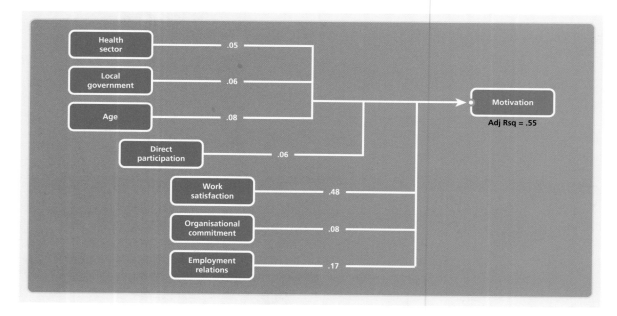

' ... levels of motivation are generally quite high; they are higher in the health and local government sectors than elsewhere ... .'

The results confirm the initial statistical analysis in showing that both health and local government workers report significantly higher motivation than private industry workers, while central government workers are no different to those in private industry. They also confirm the model of the psychological contract that links attitudes to behaviour. The three attitudinal items covering employment relations, commitment and in particular work satisfaction are all associated with higher motivation. The only other background factors that have a highly significant association are age – older workers report higher motivation – and the scope for direct participation. This last item confirms the importance of providing autonomy and scope for decision-making in the job.

Three other factors show a significant association with motivation but less strongly than some of those above. The first is the state of the

psychological contract. This indicates that it has a direct association as well as one that is mediated through the attitude items. The final two items show that ethnic minority workers and those who have dependent children are more highly motivated. There are no obvious explanations for this, although it is possible to speculate on plausible reasons.

In summary, levels of motivation are generally quite high; they are higher in the health and local government sectors than elsewhere; and there is some support for the adage that a satisfied worker is also a motivated worker.

Effort

Effort is measured with a single item asking people how hard they were working. The results are shown in Table 12.

Table 12 | Levels of effort

	Central government	Local government	Health	Industry	Total
HOW HARD WOULD YOU SAY YOU WORK? **Which of the following statements best describes your current feelings when you are at work?**					
I am not working particularly hard	4	3	2	4	3
I am working quite hard	35	26	22	31	28
I am working very hard	40	46	47	37	43
I am working as hard as I can and could not imagine working any harder	22	24	29	27	25

Note: All figures are expressed as percentages.

'... workers report generally high levels of effort, with health sector workers reporting higher levels than workers in central government and industry.'

As in previous years, most people believe they are working very hard. Health sector workers report significantly higher levels of effort than those in central government and industry. There are no other differences between the groups.

The fuller analysis of the background factors associated with different levels of effort is shown in Figure 14. Unlike motivation, only a relatively small amount of variation in effort levels is explained by the background factors. This is not surprising since if it is a function of issues like work demands and technology, then these are not covered in this survey. Looking first at the highly significant associations, positive work attitudes, and in particular commitment and work satisfaction, are associated with higher effort. However, there is a negative association with the psychological contract. This has been found in all previous surveys and may reflect a view that those who put in higher levels of effort have a more negative effort–reward bargain, which is one component of the psychological contract. Men also report lower levels of effort than women.

There are a number of other factors that have a significant influence, albeit slightly less strong. Those working in larger establishments report less effort; so do those with higher incomes and those who are single. There is no very clear explanation why these factors should appear, but it may possibly be linked in some way to other commitments in life, which could also explain why men report less effort than women. The final factor to note, perhaps not surprisingly, is that those who work longer hours report more effort. Once other factors have been taken into account, none of the core groups reports significantly more effort. However, it is worth noting that central government employees just fail to show significantly lower levels of effort than those in private industry. It seems probable that significant differences between health sector and central government employees also remain once other factors have been taken into account, but this was not directly tested.

In summary, workers report generally high levels of effort, with health sector workers reporting higher levels than workers in central government. Higher effort is linked to positive attitudes to work and to longer working hours. Women report more effort than men; and those who are single and those who have higher incomes report less effort. There is a complex link to the psychological contract, which is associated with higher motivation but lower effort.

Figure 14 | Determinants of effort

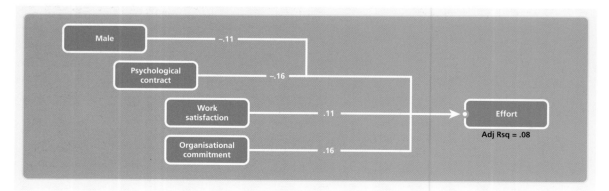

Organisational citizenship

Organisational citizenship behaviour is concerned with the extent to which people are willing to act outside their conventional role and be good citizens of the organisation. As organisations become increasingly complex, flexible and responsive, a willingness to do this may become more important to ensure that work is completed successfully. Organisational citizenship can also be seen as part of the reciprocal element of the psychological contract. In other words, it addresses the obligations or the inclinations of workers to do something for the organisation – possibly in return for what the organisation has already done for them. In this case we asked about obligations –

Table 13 | Organisational citizenship behaviour

	Central government	Local government	Health	Industry	Total
STRENGTH OF OBLIGATION TO:					
Go to work, even if you don't feel particularly well					
little obligation	16	9	8	14	12
some obligation	35	31	26	30	31
strong obligation	48	60	65	56	58
Show loyalty to the organisation					
little obligation	6	6	3	8	6
some obligation	37	28	26	28	26
strong obligation	56	66	69	63	64
Be polite to customers or the public, even if they are rude to you					
little obligation	3	2	1	5	4
some obligation	12	9	6	11	9
strong obligation	84	87	92	78	85
Work enthusiastically on jobs you would prefer not to be doing					
little obligation	6	7	3	8	5
some obligation	56	43	41	44	47
strong obligation	38	48	54	46	46
Work overtime or extra hours when required					
little obligation	19	17	14	17	17
some obligation	36	30	35	33	34
strong obligation	43	51	50	50	49
Volunteer to do tasks outside your job description					
little obligation	17	20	23	24	21
some obligation	52	42	40	39	43
strong obligation	30	35	36	34	44

Note: All figures are expressed as percentages.

the things they felt they *ought* to do – rather than things they actually wished to do. There were six topics that were covered and the responses are shown in Table 13. In the survey, workers were asked to respond on a 10-point scale from *no obligation* at one extreme (1) to *a very strong obligation* (10) at the other extreme. For the purposes of presentation, we have collapsed the 10-point scale into three categories. 'Little obligation' covers responses from 1–3; 'some obligation' covers responses from 4–7; and 'strong obligation' covers responses from 8–10. A few of the columns do not add up to 100 per cent because some questions, such as politeness to customers, were not considered to be relevant by all respondents.

A factor analysis showed that all the items could be combined into one scale, although there was some indication that the first four items deal with aspects of helpfulness while the last two tap a slightly different dimension of volunteering to do extra. For the present, we shall treat them as a single dimension of organisational citizenship behaviour.[2]

The results confirm that a majority of workers feel a strong obligation to attend work, to show loyalty and to be polite to customers. This obligation was somewhat weaker when it came to showing enthusiasm for less appealing work and volunteering for extra tasks. The results show the familiar pattern of variation among the four groups. Health sector workers are significantly more likely to report a willingness to engage in citizenship behaviour than central government and private industry workers. Local government workers are also significantly more positive than central government workers. Central government workers are again the least positive in their responses, reinforcing the importance of considering variations within the public sector.

We can determine whether these differences remain when other background factors are taken into account. The key results of the regression analysis are presented in Figure 15.

The more rigorous analysis reflected in Figure 15 shows that the differences between the four groups are no longer significant. Instead an

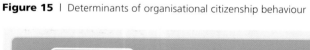

Figure 15 | Determinants of organisational citizenship behaviour

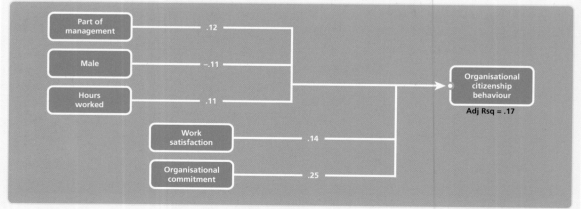

2. The alpha for the scale containing the combined items measuring obligations reflecting organisational citizenship was .70.

'The psychological contract is negatively associated with citizenship behaviour, implying that a number of workers do not believe that management appropriately recognises and rewards their extra contribution.'

additional set of factors, dominated by attitudes, explains variations in citizenship behaviour. In total, the various background factors explain about 17 per cent of the variations in responses on the citizenship measure. Other predictable factors emerge. Those who report that they are part of management are more likely to engage in citizenship behaviour. So too are those working longer hours – given that one of the items concerns willingness to work longer hours, this is hardly surprising. For some reason, men are less willing than women to behave as good citizens. In addition to the items shown in Figure 15, citizenship behaviour is also associated with a higher level of educational qualification. It is negatively associated with scope for direct participation, size of establishment and the state of the psychological contract. The finding on the psychological contract has appeared in previous surveys and may reflect the view that citizenship behaviour, the workers' side of the mutual obligations that make up the exchange in the psychological contract, has not been sufficiently reciprocated by the organisation.

In summary, while the sense of obligation to engage in citizenship behaviour is generally quite high, there are also considerable variations in response. The initial finding that health sector workers show most inclination and central government employees least inclination to engage in such behaviour does not fully hold up under more rigorous analysis. Instead, attitudes such as commitment and job satisfaction have the more significant influence and more predictable factors such as being part of management and working longer hours also show a strong association. The psychological contract is negatively associated with citizenship behaviour, implying that a number of workers do not believe that management appropriately recognises and rewards their extra contribution. Finally, it is worth bearing in mind that these items deal with the extent to which workers feel obliged to undertake certain activities. While this provides a strong indication of how they are likely to behave, and we have labelled this section organisational citizenship *behaviour*, we need to remain cautious about inferring that obligations and behaviour are synonymous.

Table 14 | Intention to leave the organisation

	Central government	Local government	Health	Industry	Total
HOW LIKELY IS IT THAT YOU WILL LEAVE THE ORGANISATION IN THE FOLLOWING YEAR?					
not at all likely	59	57	59	49	56
slightly likely	23	20	21	18	20
fairly likely	8	9	9	12	9
very likely	9	13	11	20	13
don't know	2	1	0	2	1

Note: All figures are expressed as percentages.

Intention to leave the organisation

In a tight labour market, ability to retain employees can be an important asset. Previous research has shown that intention to leave or stay with an organisation is the best predictor of subsequent turnover behaviour. We therefore asked about this. There was space to ask only one question. Reponses to that question are shown in Table 14 on page 41.

The results appear to show marked differences between the public and private sectors. One in five private industry workers say it is very likely that they will leave in the next year compared with less than one in 10 in central government. This is confirmed in a statistical comparison. People working in private industry are significantly more likely to leave than those in any of the public sector groups. At the same time, there are no significant differences within the public sector.

A fuller analysis was conducted to identify other influences on variation in likelihood of leaving. The various background factors account for 29 per cent of the variation in responses. The highly significant items are shown in Figure 16.

Figure 16 shows a wide range of influences. A minus sign indicates that the variable is associated with a lower intention to leave. The results therefore confirm that workers in central

Figure 16 | Determinants of intention to leave the organisation

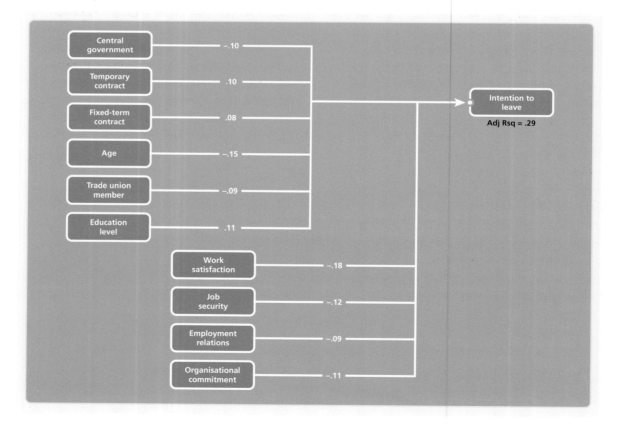

' **... while those who feel part of management and work long hours generally report more positive behaviour, men are less likely than women to report a high level of effort or obligation to engage in citizenship behaviour.'**

government are less likely to leave than those in the private sector. However, when other factors are taken into account, the differences between the private sector and health and local government are no longer significant. Attitudes also have an important influence. We should not really be surprised to find that those who are more satisfied with their work, more committed to the organisation, more secure and who perceive good employment relations are more likely to stay. So too are older workers and trade union members. In contrast, those on temporary or fixed-term contracts, quite realistically, are more likely to expect to move on within the next year. So, too, are those with higher educational qualifications, who are presumably also in a stronger position in the labour market.

In reviewing these results, it is important to bear in mind that the positive attitudes are in turn associated with a range of background factors such as the number of human resource practices, the organisational climate and scope for direct participation, as well as the state of the psychological contract. They are therefore linked to the policy and practice of the organisation. The other interesting point to note is that the propensity to leave appears to be lowest among central government workers, yet they report the lowest levels of satisfaction and commitment. This suggests either that there is a powerful ethos that encourages these workers to view the civil service as a lifelong career or they do not feel that their knowledge and skills are marketable. It is possible that a sense of being trapped contributes to the explanation of the poorer psychological contract reported by central government workers.

Summary

In this chapter we have presented evidence about four indicators of behaviour at work. As the model of the psychological contract suggests, they are all closely linked to some of the attitudinal items, although there is sometimes also a weaker link to the psychological contract and some of the background practices.

The results broadly confirm the pattern shown in the chapters on the psychological contract and on attitudes in showing central government workers to be less positive in their reported behaviour, particularly when compared with workers in the health sector, who tend to be the most positive. Yet those in central government, despite indications of disaffection, are also the least likely to indicate that they might leave the organisation.

One other finding that links to the next chapter is that while those who feel part of management and work long hours generally report more positive behaviour, men are less likely than women to report a high level of effort or obligation to engage in citizenship behaviour.

7 | Work–life balance and life satisfaction

◪ **Of the sample, 41 per cent work only their contracted hours, while 14 per cent work more than 48 hours a week.**

◪ **About three-quarters of the sample think they have a reasonable balance between work and life outside work.**

◪ **Although 57 per cent say that their organisation has some core family-friendly practices in place, there is no evidence that their use has any impact on work–life balance.**

◪ **Those who have most difficulty balancing work and the rest of life are typically managers working long hours.**

◪ **About two-thirds report high levels of satisfaction with life as a whole and only 3 per cent admit that they are very dissatisfied with it.**

There has been increasing national interest in issues concerning the balance between work and the rest of life and in the role that family-friendly policies can play in helping to promote an appropriate balance. The discussion is reinforced by evidence about the long hours of British workers and the contribution of legislation designed to limit the requirement to work more than 48 hours. This survey therefore looks at some of the issues related to work–life balance and the role of family-friendly practices. The chapter starts with an analysis of working hours, moves on to explore family-friendly practices and then examines perceptions of balance between work and the rest of life.

Working hours

59 per cent of the sample are contracted to work between 35 and under 40 hours a week. Nine per cent are contracted to work less than 20 hours a week and 19 per cent less than 30 hours per week. This indicates that the sample has a lower proportion of part-time workers than we might expect. The proportion working less than 30 hours ranges from only 8 per cent in central government to between 23 and 25 per cent in the other three sectors.

The hours actually worked are likely to be more important in determining work–life balance. The reported distribution across the four groups is shown in Table 15.

On the surface, the figures in Table 15 do not indicate a serious problem of working hours. No group is working more than 40 hours a week on average. However, the average figure is somewhat distorted by the presence of part-time workers, so it is more useful to look at some of the extremes. On this basis, we can see that 41 per cent work only their contracted hours. However, 14 per cent work more than the 48 hours deemed by the European Union to be an acceptable maximum, and 12 per cent are working at least 11 hours a week beyond those contracted. In contrast, only 2 per cent reported working fewer hours than they were contracted to work.

There are some consistent differences between the four groups. Private industry has the largest proportion working long hours. It also has the largest proportion who are working only contracted hours. It is therefore an environment of extremes. In the public sector, although there may be some well-publicised exceptions such as junior hospital doctors, most exceed contracted hours by only a small margin, if indeed they do at all.

Why do people work these longer hours? We asked whether this was something that they chose to do, felt forced to do by the circumstances at work or whether it was some combination of both. The responses are shown in Table 16. They apply only to those who said they typically worked longer than their contracted hours.

The responses indicate that about a quarter of those who work extra hours feel forced into doing so by circumstances at work, although an extra 31 per cent report that this is partly or sometimes the case. In private industry, where more people work long hours, a larger proportion also say that they do so out of personal choice. The broad implication is that in the public sector in particular, the workload and the demands of the work are causing the longer hours for most people; but for

Table 15 | Hours actually worked

	Central government	Local government	Health	Industry	Total
Average number of hours actually worked	40	36	37	39	38
% working 48+ hours	12	10	11	23	14
% working only contracted hours	36	41	43	45	41
% working 11+ hours beyond those contracted	7	13	10	17	12

Table 16 | Reasons for working longer hours

	Central government	Local government	Health	Industry	Total
n =	307	293	277	264	1141
Personal choice (%)	44	39	33	55	43
Forced to by circumstances at work (%)	25	31	29	17	26
A bit of both (%)	30	30	38	27	31

a sizeable minority it is their own choice and reflects their commitment, as indicated in some of the earlier responses.

Family-friendly policies and practices

Reactions to long hours and concern about the balance between work and the rest of life may be affected by the support and flexibility permitted by the employing organisation. Relevant practices are typically described in terms of family-friendly policies. One item within the set of human resource practices covered this. However, here we return to explore the issue in a little more detail. The subject was covered by asking, as already described, whether the organisation had any family-friendly policies. With those who answered positively, we went a step further and asked about specific practices. The responses are shown in Table 17.

Table 17 | Experience of family-friendly practices

	Central government	Local government	Health	Industry	Total
THE ORGANISATION PROVIDES SOME SORT OF SUPPORT THAT HELPS EMPLOYEES TO DEAL WITH NON-WORK RESPONSIBILITIES – IE FAMILY-FRIENDLY POLICIES SUCH AS CHILDCARE, COUNSELLING FOR NON-WORK PROBLEMS, FINANCIAL AND LEGAL SERVICES.					
Yes	77	52	63	34	57
No	20	41	34	60	39
Don't know	4	6	3	6	5
DOES YOUR ORGANISATION OFFER: (% SAYING YES)					
Time off for family illness	87	77	78	71	78
Opportunities to vary formal hours	88	65	69	50	68
Opportunities to work at home from time to time	50	32	26	21	32
Advice and support services in case of pressures and conflicts between work and home	70	55	60	35	55
HAVE YOU USED THE OPPORTUNITY? (% SAYING YES)					
Time off for family illness	35	29	27	32	31
Opportunities to vary formal hours	64	64	55	67	62
Opportunities to work at home from time to time	46	57	60	77	56
Advice and support services in case of pressures and conflicts between work and home	15	12	13	17	14

We have provided only a small list of family-friendly practices and omitted items such as crèche facilities, since these would be relevant to only some of the respondents. The responses indicate that industry lags well behind the public sector in general, and central government in particular, in its provision of the specific practices listed in the first question and also the more flexible working arrangements presented in Table 17. Indeed, there is a consistent picture whereby central government offers the greatest provision followed some way behind by local government and the health sector, which in turn is followed by private industry.

When it comes to actual take-up of practices, the differences largely disappear. Indeed, workers in private industry are among the heavier users, more particularly of the opportunity to work from home from time to time. More generally, those with dependent children are more likely to use them. So, too, are those on temporary contracts, multiple job-holders and those working longer hours. Blue-collar workers are rather less likely to use them, along with those on a higher income and those who are single. It would appear that the provision of flexible work arrangements should ease the balance between the demands of home and work. The next section explores the nature of this balance and then examines whether family-friendly practices contribute to a better balance.

The balance between work and life outside work

The concept of work–life balance is widely and loosely applied. It implies a weighing of one part of life against others, which may be inappropriate for those whose work blends into the rest of their life. It ignores the fact that work is often a central part of life. It needs to consider individual differences in preferences; and, bearing in mind responses to the earlier question about reasons for working longer hours, it needs to reflect scope for choice. The following section should be read with these provisos in mind.

The first central issue is whether people believe they have the right balance between work and their life outside work. Responses are shown in Table 18.

The results are reasonably consistent across the four groups. Approximately three-quarters of the working population say they have the right balance between home and work. This still leaves a quarter who have the wrong balance and raises

Table 18 | The balance between work and life outside work

	Central government	Local government	Health	Industry	Total
DO YOU THINK YOU HAVE THE RIGHT BALANCE BETWEEN WORK AND YOUR LIFE OUTSIDE WORK?					
Yes	72	77	73	71	74
No	27	22	26	28	26

Note: All figures are expressed as percentages.

questions about who these people are. Before examining this, we need to confirm the popular assumption that an imbalance is caused by too much work. Those who reported an imbalance were asked whether work or life outside work dominates. As expected, 91 per cent said that work dominates.

We conducted a regression analysis[1] to determine the factors associated with a positive work–life balance. The results are presented in Figure 17. In this chapter, we are particularly interested in the range of influences. We therefore include in this

and subsequent figures all the significant associations. The asterisks show the level of significance (* = significant at the 5% level; ** = significant at the 1% level; *** = significant at the .1% level).

A large number of background factors help to explain whether or not someone reports the right balance between work and life outside work. However, in total they account for only 14 per cent of the variation in responses. This is not surprising since a number of non-work factors that we were unable to measure probably have an important

Figure 17 | Determinants of balance between work and the rest of life

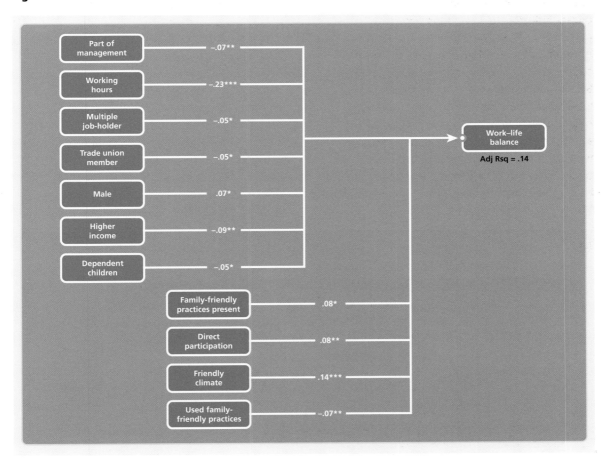

1. Strictly speaking, with a dichotomous dependent variable we should be conducting logistic regression. We did in fact conduct this analysis and found virtually identical results to those obtained with a conventional linear regression. Since it is easier to present the results of the latter in terms of standard beta weights, it is this that we use in the report.

influence. Even in the results in Figure 17 we can see some influence of non-work factors; for example, women and those with dependent children are more likely to report an unsatisfactory balance. However, a number of work-related factors are also important. Predictably, the most important of these is working hours, with those working longer hours reporting a poorer balance. However, there are ameliorating factors, including a friendly working climate, more human resource practices and greater autonomy in the job, reflected in direct participation. Local government workers also report a better balance than those in industry. A poorer balance is associated with being a part of management, being a trade union member and holding multiple jobs. More surprisingly, it is also associated with a higher income.

Family-friendly practices have a complex link to work–life balance. While the presence of such practices appears to be positive, use of them is associated with a poorer balance. It appears from this that for the heavier users of these practices – those with dependent children, those in multiple jobs and those working long hours – family-friendly practices either fail to reduce the imbalance or at least fail to do so sufficiently to lead these workers to report a satisfactory balance. By implication, such practices are, at best, a palliative rather than a cure for the problem of work–life imbalance.

In summary, the evidence suggests that there are some features of roles at home and at work that make it more difficult to achieve a satisfactory balance, but that in addition features of the work environment make a difference – a positive environment, reflected in a friendly climate, the presence of family-friendly practices and greater job autonomy are all associated with a better balance.

Even if there is an acceptable balance between work and life outside work, it is possible that work may still get in the way of life outside. Responses to a question exploring this showed a very similar pattern of results across the four groups. 14 per cent said this happened most of the time, 35 per cent said it happened some of the time and 34 per cent said it happened not very often. The remaining 17 per cent said it never

Table 19 | Work as a central life interest

	Central government	Local government	Health	Industry	Total
THINKING ABOUT YOUR LIFE AT WORK AND YOUR LIFE OUTSIDE WORK (SUCH AS FRIENDS, HOBBIES, LEISURE ACTIVITIES AND FAMILY) WOULD YOU SAY YOU ARE MORE COMMITTED TO:					
work	13	10	12	19	14
equally committed to both	59	64	62	54	60
life outside work	28	22	25	27	25

Note: All figures are expressed as percentages.

> ' … we should be cautious in inferring that people wish to separate work from the rest of their lives. A willingness to accept overlap may be found in particular among those who consider that work is, at least in part, a central life interest.'

happened. What this suggests is that it is common for work to get in the way of life outside work from time to time and that this is accepted as relatively normal.

Further support for this comes from responses to an item considered briefly earlier in the report. 61 per cent indicated that they keep work separate from the rest of their lives most of the time. This varied between 65 per cent in central government and 56 per cent in local government. At the other extreme, 15 per cent said this was rarely or never possible. This again varied between 17 per cent in local government and 13 per cent in central government. Younger workers appear to find it easier to keep the two worlds separate. Despite the debates on working hours and the growing demands of work, we should be cautious in inferring that people wish to separate work from the rest of their lives. A willingness to accept overlap may be found in particular among those who consider that work is, at least in part, a central life interest.

Work as a central life interest

Concern about an imbalance between work and the rest of life depends partly on which is the most important sphere of life. Over the years there has been much research on work as a central interest in life. In this year's survey, we explored this through an item asking whether people were more committed to work, to life outside work or to both equally. The responses are shown in Table 19 on page 50.

These results confirm the importance of a balance between work and the rest of life and suggest that a balance means giving weight to both. A quarter report greater commitment to life outside work while only 14 per cent report that they are more committed to work. There are some minor differences between the groups, with those in industry tending to lie at both extremes. These results are very different from those obtained when an identical question was asked in 1996. In that year, 22 per cent said they were more committed to work, 23 per cent were more committed to life outside work and 55 per cent were equally committed to both. While the sample may have been slightly different in make-up, there is still evidence of a marked shift away from work as a dominant central life interest. This may be a result of the greater prominence given to issues of work–life balance in the last year or two or it may represent a real retreat from the excessive demands of work. Whatever the underlying causes, it reflects an important shift in work-related values.

We can identify those who are more likely to express commitment to work or to life outside work through a conventional regression analysis. The results are shown in Figure 18. A positive link indicates more commitment to life outside work; a negative sign indicates more commitment to work.

The results contain some predictable responses and some surprises. Those more committed to life outside work are likely to have dependent children, to be male and to have higher educational qualifications. Those more committed to work are those who work longer hours (suggesting that the longer hours often reflect the fact that they are more committed to their work), those who are older, part of management, in settings with a dynamic climate and scope for direct participation and those on fixed-term contracts. Work is also more likely to be a central life interest for those from ethnic minorities and those who are divorced. Neither of these findings is particularly surprising. The background influences account for only 12 per cent of the variation in responses. However, they do serve to highlight the link between long hours and commitment to work as well as a number of other fairly predictable associations. Personal circumstances have an important bearing on the centrality of work; nevertheless, one of the least expected findings is that men are more likely than women to report a stronger commitment to life outside work.

Those who are more committed to work are likely to behave differently at work. For example, they display significantly higher levels of motivation and they are more likely to feel obliged to engage in organisational citizenship behaviours. Returning for a moment to the question of balance, this can also be linked to certain aspects of behaviour at work. Those who report a good balance between work and life outside work are less likely to report high effort demands at work and are less likely to feel that they have to engage in organisational citizenship behaviour. Since organisational citizenship behaviour was also associated with a poorer psychological contract, it appears that it is perceived by those who are not highly committed

Figure 18 I Determinants of work as a central life interest

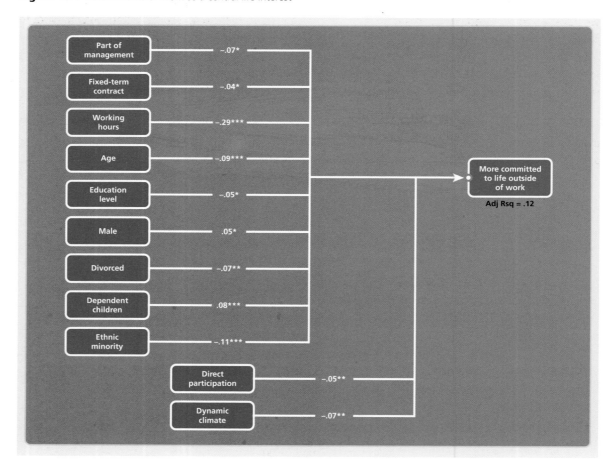

to work as an extra and unreasonable demand – in other words, for many workers it is an obligation rather than behaviour that is entirely voluntary.

Life satisfaction

The exploration of work–life balance and work as a central life interest has shifted the focus to issues that transcend the work environment. In this final section of the chapter, we examine issues of life satisfaction. Questions about life satisfaction have been covered in previous surveys, so a later chapter will explore some of the comparisons over time. Here we concentrate initially on comparisons between the key groups of workers. The interview asked about several aspects of life, some of which we have already covered. Responses to the seven items are summarised in Table 20. Responses were given on a scale from totally dissatisfied (1) to totally satisfied (10). Table 20 shows the average scores for the relevant groups

The responses indicate that on every item workers in central government report lower levels of satisfaction than the other three groups. At the other extreme, health sector workers are more satisfied on all items, closely followed by local government workers. A statistical comparison across the combined items confirms that health sector workers are more satisfied with life as a whole than central government and private industry workers, while local government workers are also more satisfied than those in central government. If we look just at the single item on satisfaction with work–life balance, central government workers are again significantly less satisfied than those in both the health sector and local government.

We can look more generally at the background factors that are associated with life satisfaction. In this case, we should expect factors outside work to exert some sort of influence. The results for the regression analysis of factors associated with life satisfaction as a whole, which is a measure combining the items in Table 20, is shown in Figure 19. We have excluded the attitudinal and behavioural items outlined in the two previous chapters from this analysis.

Table 20 | Life satisfaction

	Central government	Local government	Health	Industry	Total
Your life as a whole	7.61	7.97	8.05	7.69	7.83
Your family and friends	8.50	8.78	8.93	8.69	8.73
Your health	7.94	8.16	8.27	8.16	8.13
Your finances	6.22	6.47	6.47	6.33	6.37
Your work	6.69	7.16	7.54	6.99	7.10
Your employer	6.43	6.90	7.04	6.68	6.73
Balance between work and life outside work	6.78	7.19	7.20	6.84	7.00

'Health sector workers report significantly more satisfaction with life as a whole compared with those in industry ... .'

The analysis shows that there is a strong association between life satisfaction and the state of the psychological contract. Since there is also an association with the two dimensions of organisational climate, this confirms that the experience of work has an important link to life satisfaction. There is also evidence that the organisational setting and work role makes a difference. Health sector workers report significantly more satisfaction with life as a whole compared with those in industry; although the direct comparison was not made in this analysis, they will also be more satisfied than central government workers. Those in white-collar and blue-collar jobs as opposed to management jobs are also more satisfied. On the negative side, those on temporary contracts and more particularly those working long hours report less satisfaction with life as a whole. Moving outside work, those who are single, divorced and who have dependent children are less satisfied. By implication, those who are married but have no dependent children

Figure 19 | Determinants of life satisfaction

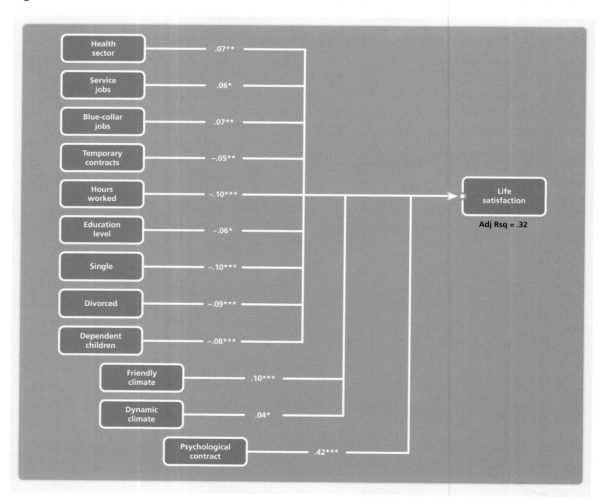

are the most satisfied. Less obviously, those with higher educational qualifications are also less satisfied with life as a whole.

The final issue we return to is the level of satisfaction with the balance between work and life outside work. We have already addressed this indirectly by asking whether people believe they have the right balance between work and life outside work. The responses are summarised in Figure 20.

The results are similar to those presented in Figure 17. A major difference is that the measure of the psychological contract is included in this second analysis and emerges as highly significant. More generally it confirms the importance of working hours in contributing to dissatisfaction with the balance and also the challenges created by having dependent children. Family-friendly practices do not seem to alleviate the pressures caused by dependent children.

Figure 20 | Satisfaction with balance between work and the rest of life

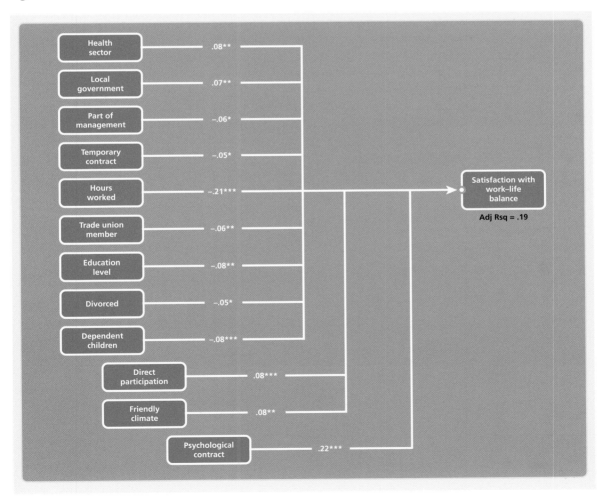

> 'One of the consistent findings ... is that health sector workers are more satisfied and central government workers less satisfied than those in the other employment groups.'

Summary

This chapter has covered various aspects of the balance between work and life outside work. For an important minority there is an imbalance that is associated with the demands of work, reflected in long hours and the responsibility associated with being part of management. It is also affected by circumstances outside work, including marital status and dependent children.

One of the consistent findings in this and other chapters is that health sector workers are more satisfied and central government workers less satisfied than those in the other employment groups. This raises a question of whether the pattern of responses reflects a generalised response. In other words, some disaffection with aspects of work experience colours responses to all aspects of working life and life beyond work. Taking this a step further, it is possible to argue that responses throughout the survey tap some generalised level of satisfaction or dissatisfaction. However, this fails to explain why those in central government should be consistently more negative and those in the health sector consistently more positive. We shall return to this issue when we examine differences within each of the groups.

8 | Change at work

◘ **Change at work has become part of organisational life. 55 per cent said their organisation had gone through a major change during the past year.**

◘ **Organisational change is associated with a poorer psychological contract, less job security and poorer worker–management relations.**

◘ **Redundancies and staff reductions have a consistently negative impact on those who stay, but new technology and team-building activities are more positively received.**

◘ **If they could choose a change, workers would opt for conventional choices – more pay, a reduced workload and promotion/advancement.**

Change at work has become the common experience for many workers. This does not necessarily make it any more welcome. There are constant complaints about too much change, about the pace of change and about the excessive demands placed on workers by the way in which change is managed. Cynics argue that there is too much change for the sake of change or to enable senior managers to make their mark. Much of this is speculation and we need a clearer account of how workers perceive change and what consequences they believe it has for them. The report on the 1999 IPD survey provides some detailed analysis of this topic.[1] Here we pick up just some of the issues, starting with reports of the amount of change being experienced, looking at the type of change, assessing reactions to change and finally considering the kinds of change that workers themselves would welcome.

The experience of change

55 per cent of the sample said that their organisation had been going through some sort of major change during the last year. This confirms

the belief that major change is becoming a common feature of working life. The figure ranged from 65 per cent in central government to 48 per cent in private industry. The figures for local government and the health sector were 54 per cent and 51 per cent respectively. These figures challenge the assumption that change is a particular feature of a dynamic private industry.

We can obtain more detail of the contexts and types of worker most affected through a regression analysis. The results are shown in Figure 21. This reveals that a large number of background factors have a significant but not a major influence on the experience of change and that together they account for a modest 6 per cent of the variation in responses. The only highly significant background factor is organisational size; those working in larger organisations are more likely to report major change in the last year. The other factors associated with reports of more change are being a part of management, having higher educational qualifications and being a trade union member. It is possible that these attributes may help to heighten awareness of change. Some

1. *Organisational Change and the Psychological Contract*, to be published by the CIPD near the end of 2000.

individual factors are associated with lower reports of change; these range from being in blue-collar and clerical jobs as opposed to management jobs, being on temporary and fixed-term contracts, which means that there has been less time to experience change, and more idiosyncratically, being single or a member of an ethnic minority.

Figure 21 | Determinants of organisational change

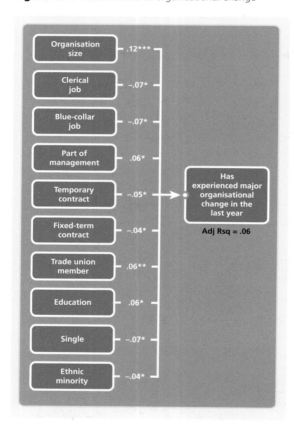

The content of change

We offered a list of seven types of change. The figures in Table 21 show which were considered by workers to have occurred in their organisations. These responses apply only to those who reported that some sort of change had taken place.

These responses indicate that the types of change vary widely covering in particular reorganisation, change in management style and new technology. Mergers and takeovers are much more common in the private sector and in health, where the mergers among trusts are affecting many people. Redundancies and staff reductions are also more likely to have occurred in the private sector. New technology is being introduced fairly evenly across the sectors. The public sector and more particularly central government has emphasised programmes of culture change, but all sectors are apparently extensively engaged in reorganisation of work and changes in leadership and management style.

Reactions to change might be affected by the amount of change. Among those reporting change, 60 per cent reported only one or two changes, 34 per cent reported between three and five of them, and 6 per cent reported six or all seven of the changes occurring in the last year.

Reactions to change

We did not ask direct questions about reactions to change. However, it was possible to link the experience of change to the various attitudinal and behavioural outcomes that were discussed in earlier chapters and determine whether the changes had any influence on the responses above and beyond those already accounted for by other background factors.

'The greater the number of changes, the more negative the
impact on the friendly climate, the psychological contract
and job security.'

We can examine whether the experience of change had any impact. One area where we might expect to see an impact is the organisational climate. Those reporting change described their climate as less friendly than those not experiencing change. However, even though change might be seen as an indication of dynamism, there was no significant link between the experience of change and a more dynamic climate.

In general, the experience of change is associated with more negative attitudes. For example, those who have reported change in the last year have a poorer psychological contract, feel less secure and consider employment relations to be poorer. When we look at the impact of the amount of change a similar picture emerges. The greater the number of changes, the more negative the impact on the friendly climate, the psychological contract and job security. The link to employment relations is negative no matter what the level of change and does not seem to vary much. There is no link between the amount of change and a more or less dynamic climate or to other aspects of job satisfaction and behaviour. However, there is a hint

that a small amount of change does improve life satisfaction.

To make sense of this we need to explore in more detail reactions to the specific types of change. In the meantime, we can conclude that in general change has a negative impact on a number of key attitudes, the greater the amount of change, the greater the negative impact and there is little sign of any positive general impact.

Reactions to specific types of change

Some of the types of change listed can be expected to have a more negative impact than others. Some of the 'softer' changes are usually intended to have a positive impact on employee attitudes and behaviour. To assess this, we looked at the impact of each type of change in turn.

The result confirms a differential impact. As might be expected, the experience of redundancy and staff reductions has a consistently negative impact, particularly on feelings of job security, the state of the psychological contract and perceptions of

Table 21 | The content of change (% who have experienced each type of change in the past year)

	Central government	Local government	Health	Industry	Total
A merger/takeover	8	13	42	55	28
Redundancies/reductions in staff	25	42	34	47	36
Reorganisation of your work	67	69	58	63	64
Leadership/management style	70	65	69	67	68
Culture change	60	43	43	39	47
Teambuilding/the way you work with colleagues	54	48	53	46	50
New technology	68	69	59	59	64

whether the climate is friendly, but also on employment relations and commitment. Reorganisations tend to have a negative impact on the state of the psychological contract and on the extent to which the climate is perceived as dynamic. Leadership change has no significant impact on attitudes and behaviour, and culture change has an impact – a negative impact – only on perceptions of whether the climate is friendly. New technology, which might be expected to have a more positive impact, is associated with a more friendly climate but not with any attitudes or behaviours. Finally, team-building is associated with a more friendly and dynamic climate. In summary, the specific changes are more likely to have their main impact on aspects of organisational climate and on the state of the psychological contract. The direction of the change is largely what we might expect, with redundancies having a negative impact and team-building and changes in working relationships being received more positively.

Desired changes

A final question about change asked each worker about the single most important thing that would improve their work life in the next year. This does not imply organisational change on any major scale, but can provide some insight into where workers' priorities lie. The five most frequently mentioned items are shown in Table 22.

The responses provide a conventional 'wish list', with more pay and benefits well out in front. The impact of the heavy workload and the desire to reduce it is also strongly to the fore. Advancement, which might be a route to more pay and benefits, is still highly valued and receives particular emphasis among central government employees. There are minor variations between the four groups; interestingly in industry, where the hours are longest, rather more emphasis is given to increased pay and benefits and slightly less to reduced workload and shorter working hours.

Summary

Change at work is pervasive. Reactions to change tend to be negative rather than positive and the greater the amount of change, the more negative the response. The type of change does have some impact on reactions. Redundancy and workforce reductions have the most negative impact, while team-building and related activities have a more positive influence on attitudes and perceptions.

Table 22 I Desired changes

	Central government	Local government	Health	Industry	Total
More pay and benefits	28	25	29	33	29
Reduced workload or shorter hours	11	11	14	8	11
Promotion and advancement	13	8	7	8	9
Increased job security	5	7	6	9	7
More training and development	4	8	8	5	6

Note: All figures are expressed as percentages.

9 | Differences within each sector

- ▣ **Central government employees are consistently more negative than others.**

- ▣ **Health sector workers are consistently the most positive.**

- ▣ **Generally, there are only minor differences between sub-sectors within any of the four main sectors in the study.**

In the analysis so far, we have compared the responses of those working in central government, local government, the health sector and industry. In this penultimate chapter of results, we explore differences within each sector. The additional feature is that we can include in the analysis some distinctive features of each sector.

Central government

In central government, the additional information concerns the groups of departments. We compared the responses of four very broad groups: those working in ministerial departments (285), in agencies (85), in non-ministerial departments (63) and in a group that included the Scottish Office and miscellaneous 'other' departments that, for convenience, we simply label 'other' departments (67). We also compared those who work in London with those employed elsewhere in the country. To determine whether these variables have any independent effects, we also retain the other background factors in the analysis.

The results suggest that these additional factors play only a relatively minor role. In the main analysis, we compared the three sets of departments against the agencies. Looking first at what might be termed the background factors – which in the model are used to explain variations in the psychological contract – there are no

differences in human resource practices. This is what we would expect. Staff in the 'other' departments report a more friendly and dynamic working climate than the agencies and also more scope for direct participation or autonomy.

Staff in the 'other' departments report a more positive psychological contract than the agencies. However, there are no differences in most work-related attitudes. The exception is commitment, which is significantly lower in the central departments than in the agencies, the differences being quite strong. Turning to aspects of behaviour, staff in the central departments and in the 'other' departments report higher levels of motivation than agency staff. In contrast, staff in all departments tend to report lower levels of effort than agency staff; the differences are significant for those in non-ministerial departments and the 'other' departments. No other differences emerge on any items in the survey.

There are few significant differences between those who work in London and elsewhere. The only issues to emerge show that London staff believe their working environment is less dynamic but more secure.

Although it is dangerous to draw any general conclusions from these rather small sub-groups, one possible inference from the rather more positive responses of the 'other' department staff is that there is a stronger identity in some of the smaller departments that end up being grouped together. This would be supported by the often more negative attitudes expressed by those who belong to large and potentially amorphous organisations.

Local government

In local government, there were two fairly large groups of workers in the sample. 158, consisting largely of teachers, worked in education and 72 worked in social services. The next largest groups were 29 in leisure and recreation and 23 in planning applications. We therefore compared the responses of those in education and social services against all the other local government employees, while still controlling for other background factors such as age, income and size of establishment.

Those in education reported fewer human resource practices in place but also reported that the organisational climate was significantly more friendly and more dynamic than that reported by those in the other local government departments. Social services workers also reported a more friendly organisational climate. The only significant difference on any attitudes and aspects of behaviour was that those in education reported a poorer balance between work and the rest of their lives.

Health

The sample in the health sector included 208 working in some aspect of management or administration, 183 in nursing and 67 in medicine and professions allied to medicine. There was a small residual group including scientists and presumably some porters, although this last group may be under-represented in the sample.

We compared the responses of those in nursing and medicine against those in management and administration. Both nursing and medical staff report significantly lower levels of direct participation; medical staff also report a less friendly organisational climate than those in management and administration and the result for nurses on this item falls just short of statistical significance. There are no significant differences in work-related attitudes and behaviour. The only other difference to emerge is that those in nursing report lower levels of life satisfaction.

Industry

We made a broad comparison across the main industrial sectors, while controlling for other factors. This revealed no statistically significant differences on any of the background, attitudinal or behavioural items.

Summary

We have now compared for any differences among broad bands within each of the sectors. In general, any differences have been modest. This suggests that there are either sector effects, as noted throughout the report, or effects at a more specific level of analysis such as age, establishment size or experience of organisational policy and practice.

10 | Changes in attitudes over the years

This survey has been undertaken annually since 1995. In this final section, we explore any trends in attitudes and in other responses. Each year we have attempted to retain a core set of items to provide a basis for comparison. This year we made more minor changes to a number of items, so those on which we can make direct comparisons are limited. Realistic comparisons are also made more difficult by the nature of the sample, with its preponderance of public sector workers. It is also important to bear in mind that the 2000 sample focuses on distinct parts of the public sector, whereas previous surveys covered the whole of the public sector in a much more random way. These caveats are simply a way of saying that the comparisons should be treated with caution.

The relevant comparisons are shown in Table 23. Most cover only the years 1998 and 2000. A few also cover 1996. Not all the human resource practices and forms of direct participation are shown. In all cases, a higher score represents a more positive score.

There are only a few items on which there has been a significant change over time. These are indicated on the right-hand side of the table. In general, they suggest that attitudes in the public sector have been getting slightly more positive over the period. Trends in the private sector are a little more mixed. Responses on the commitment items show some sort of peak in 1998. Reported levels of loyalty increased significantly between 1996 and 1998 and although they have begun to fall away again, they are still significantly above 1996 levels. In contrast, how proud you are to tell people who you work for rose only a little between 1996 and 1998 and has fallen away a little more sharply since. There is no real evidence of any change in satisfaction with the balance between work and the rest of life. However, one general indicator of interest is the positive shift in overall life satisfaction, which shows a significant improvement for both public and private sector workers between 1998 and 2000.

' ... one general indicator of interest is the positive shift in overall life satisfaction, which shows a significant improvement for both public and private sector workers between 1998 and 2000.'

Table 23 | Changes in attitudes over time

Change	1996		1998		2000		
	Public	Private	Public	Private	Public	Private	
Serious attempt to make jobs as interesting and varied as possible (% yes)	59	59	53	54	68	55	Pub. +***
Organisation actively carries out equal opportunity policies (% yes)			95	88	95	86	
I can carry out work in the way I think best[1]			3.86	3.82	3.82	3.75	
I vary how I do my work			3.11	3.04	3.11	2.93	
I choose the assignments I work on			2.34	2.36	2.30	2.27	
How much do you trust the organisation to keep its promises and commitments?	2.86	2.93	3.02	3.01	2.97	3.00	
How much loyalty would you say you feel towards the organisation you work for as a whole?	3.12	3.18	3.44	3.31	3.36	3.32	Pub.+*** Pri.+**
Are you proud to tell people who you work for?	2.92	2.93	3.08	2.99	2.89	2.84	Pub.–* Pri.–*
How motivated do you feel in your present job?			3.18	3.16	3.23	3.11	
When you get up in the morning, how often do you really look forward to going to work?			2.50	2.37	2.44	2.26	
How would you rate relations between employees and management at your organisation?	2.52	2.60	2.59	2.65	2.55	2.64	
SATISFACTION WITH:							
Life as a whole[2]			7.43	7.34	7.88	7.69	Pub.+** Pri.+**
Health			7.95	7.84	8.12	8.16	Pri.+*
Finances			6.41	6.32	6.39	6.33	
Work			7.12	6.87	7.13	6.99	
The right balance between work and life outside work (% yes)			75	73	75	71	
More committed to work (%)	18	23			13	19	
to both equally (%)	59	53			62	54	
to life outside work (%)	23	23			25	27	

1. The next set of items are all scored on a 1–4 scale, with the higher score representing a more positive response.
2. The next four items are scored on a scale from 1 to 10, with 10 indicating very high satisfaction.

11 | Discussion and conclusions

- ◪ **More human resource practices, direct participation and a positive organisational climate are all associated with a better psychological contract.**

- ◪ **Central government workers report the most human resource practices and the most direct participation, but the worst psychological contract and the lowest level of satisfaction with both work and life in general.**

- ◪ **Many people seem resigned to accept that work will sometimes get in the way of life outside work.**

- ◪ **Most people report high levels of satisfaction with life as a whole. Life satisfaction is higher among those who are married but have no dependent children, slightly lower among those with dependent children but lowest of all among those who are divorced or separated.**

The key focus in this year's survey has been on the state of the psychological contract and the employment relationship in the public sector and the extent to which British workers achieve a satisfactory balance between work and the rest of their lives. The report has also addressed issues of change at work and more generally allows us to make general comments both about the model that forms the core of the analysis and the implications of the findings for the state of employee satisfaction and well-being among British workers in 2000.

The survey sample

The analysis of public sector workers and the comparison with those in the private sector revealed a number of interesting findings. It showed that public sector workers in general, but central government workers in particular, reported a higher number of human resource practices and more scope for direct participation compared with their private sector counterparts. Both variables are strongly associated with a positive psychological contract across the sample as a whole. But for central government workers this is not the case. When we look at their perceptions and attitudes, they are consistently the most negative. With respect to the psychological contract, they believe that they have been made more promises but that fewer have been delivered in full. They believe they are treated less fairly than others and they report lower levels of trust, more particularly in their senior management. This 'central government factor' holds true even after taking into account type of work, level in the organisation and issues such as size of establishment. Furthermore, there are few differences across the various parts of central government. This raises the interesting question of what is happening to explain this phenomenon. One possibility is the process of organisational change. Central government employees report more of it than other sectors. It may be that the long-term and uncertain process of change has destabilised the old order without as yet putting anything in its place. However, this can be no more than speculation.

In contrast to the central government workers, those in the health sector were consistently more positive in their responses. This may be partly influenced by the inclusion of some workers from private nursing homes, but since private sector workers in general were not notably more positive, this seems unlikely. So once again, there seems to be a 'health sector factor' at play. Given common complaints about morale in the health services, this is an unexpected finding and may be partly attributable to the heavy investment in the sector and a sense that the future looks more positive and certain. Again, however, this is speculation.

We have said relatively little about local government. One reason for this is that workers in this sector rarely gave an extreme response at either the most positive or negative end of the continuum. Private industry appears to be behind the public sector in many of its practices. However, this may be deceptive since the range seemed to be much wider; for example, the private sector seems to include the most and the least enthusiastic and committed workers. By implication, therefore, there is considerable variation within both the public and private sectors and dangers in treating either as in any way homogeneous.

Work–life balance and life satisfaction

The second core issue explored in the survey has been the balance between work and the rest of life. Despite the longer working hours, 74 per cent said that they were comfortable with their balance between work and life outside work. However, working hours are important – they are the strongest factor explaining why some people have the wrong balance. Other corporate policies and practices help to ensure a comfortable balance. These include human resource practices, the organisational climate and scope for direct participation. Family-friendly practices are widely reported, more particularly in the public sector. But the existence and use of family-friendly practices do not in themselves make much difference to work–life balance. Nevertheless, there are hints about their potential importance. For example, women and those with dependent children are more likely to report an unsatisfactory balance. It is possible that we did not investigate sufficiently closely the family-friendly practices most salient for parents with dependent children. But the failure of the use of family-friendly practices to show any association with better work–life balance raises concerns about their efficacy.

Many workers appear to be resigned to the demands of long hours at work. 14 per cent work more than 48 hours a week on average, with those in industry leading the way. Among those working longer hours, 43 per cent overall, rising to 55 per cent in industry, say it is their own choice; they have joined the long-hours culture. About half the sample said that work gets in the way of life outside work either some of the time or most of the time; and when there is competition between home and work, work invariably wins. On the other hand, a quarter, more likely to be found in the public sector, feel forced to work extra hours by circumstances at work. There is then something of a split between those, often found in industry, who accept the long-hours culture and others, more likely to be found in the public sector and sometimes not working such long hours, who resent the imbalance in their lives but do not as yet find much help from family-friendly polices and practices.

In the sample as a whole, one of the striking findings is a decline in the proportion who consider work to be a central life interest. While this may reflect something of a culture shift, stimulated by the debate on work–life balance, it is still notable that while in 1996 22 per cent said work was more important than life outside work, this had fallen to 14 per cent in 2000. Part of this fall is a function of the sample – work is a dominant interest for 19 per cent of those in industry, but only about 12 per cent of those in the public sector – but it is a significant change nonetheless.

Work is still an important part of the overall equation determining life satisfaction. While satisfaction is greatest in the non-work spheres of family and friends and personal health, work in general is a greater source of satisfaction than the workers' employer or their personal finances. There are some notable differences within the sample. Across every aspect of life satisfaction, central government workers report the lowest responses. This raises issues of some spillover effect from the reported disaffection with work. Second, and as might be expected, personal circumstances make a difference. Among the most satisfied with life as a whole are married couples with no dependent children. Those with dependent children as well as those who are single and more particularly separated or divorced are less satisfied. This variation in levels of life satisfaction does not emerge in evaluations of specific satisfaction with work, where work-based issues tend to be more important, despite the provisos about central government employees noted above.

Organisational change

One of the unsurprising findings is the pervasiveness of organisational change. However, the very fact that it is now commonplace might be expected to limit its impact as people learn to live with it. While workers in central government report more change, it is likely to be in the 'soft' areas like culture change rather than mergers and staff cutbacks that are most likely to result in a negative reaction. Indeed, it is important to avoid generalisations about organisational change. While the types of change just noted – mergers, staff cutbacks and redundancies – are invariably damaging to employees' attitudes and behaviour, others, such as efforts at team-building and the introduction of new technology may be much more positively received. However, the change process needs to be carefully managed and one of the general lessons from the study is that those who report lots of change over the last year across a whole range of issues are likely to be more negative in their attitudes.

The state of the psychological contract

At the heart of the analysis in this year and others is the assessment of the state of the psychological contract and the employment relationship. As in previous years, the state of the psychological contract and the employment relationship more generally can be described as moderately positive. For example, 64 per cent say they are 'definitely' or 'probably' fairly rewarded for the amount of effort they put into their job and 58 per cent report relations between workers and management to be 'excellent' or 'good'. Once again, the model appears to work very well. This

> ' ... the employment relationship is in reasonably good shape
> in British industry. However, there is still a significant group
> of workers who remain disaffected.'

can be summarised in Figure 22. This brings
together some of the key links that were described
in the previous chapters. Of course, we must be
careful about assuming causality. This is a cross-
sectional study. Nevertheless, the 1999 analysis,
which contained a longitudinal element, showed
that the causal assumptions embedded in the
model are probably generally valid. In other words,
the 'causal' factors do help to shape assessments
of the state of the psychological contract, which in
turn affects attitudes and then behaviour. This has
important policy implications; organisations need
to ensure that they have in place policies to
promote the use of progressive human resource
practices, that ensure a degree of direct
participation and a friendly climate.

Changes in attitudes

The analysis of changes over time indicates little
shift in attitudes. There are potential problems in
direct comparisons because of the distinctive
sample used this year. However, by comparing
pubic and private sector employees over the three
years of 1996, 1998 and 2000, we can identify
few clear trends.

We have discussed differences between sectors
but given rather less attention to other
background characteristics. The results confirm the
results of other studies in showing that those
working in larger organisations and to a lesser
extent in larger establishments tend to be less

Figure 22 | The summary of the role of the psychological contract

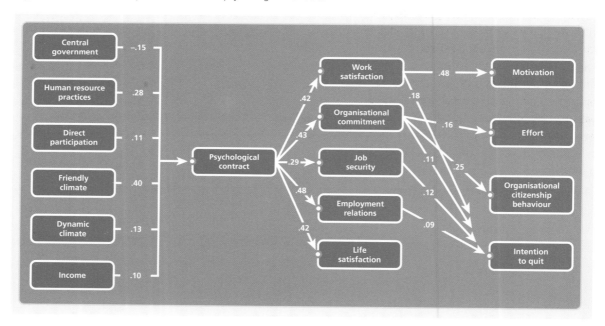

satisfied with life at work. A more consistent finding is that trade union members are invariably more discontented or negative in their assessments. Since this finding emerges after controlling for other factors such as type of work and income, it suggests either that there is something about those who choose to join a union or something about the experience of being a union member that affects attitudes. For example, trade union members may pay more attention to promises and their delivery or they may have higher expectations. This is not a new finding but it is not a well-understood one and deserves further attention.

Summary

The results confirm that the employment relationship is in reasonably good shape in British industry. However, there is still a significant group of workers who remain disaffected; a number, particularly in central government, who believe that their psychological contract is being breached; and many who are working long hours with varying degrees of enthusiasm and tolerance for what it does to their lives.

Appendix 1

Descriptive summary of background variables used in the analysis

Background variable	Category	Percentage of sample
Number of paying jobs	One	93.9
	Two	5.4
	Three	.5
	Four or more	.2
Number of employees at same location	Fewer than 10 employees	11.6
	10–24 employees	16.3
	25–99 employees	25.1
	100–499 employees	25.8
	500–999 employees	6.6
	1,000 or more employees	14.6
Total number of employees in organisation	10–24 employees	4.4
	25–99 employees	9.0
	100–499 employees	15.2
	500–999 employees	7.9
	1,000 or more employees	63.5
Sector	A company (one that is privately owned)	24.9
	The National Health Service or healthcare	25.2
	Central government	25.0
	Local government, including the police	24.9
Type of work	Director, senior manager (eg departmental or section manager/administrator)	9.4
	Other manager (eg store/shop/sales manager, office or facility manager)	14.5
	Professional (eg doctor, lawyer, chartered accountant, teacher, architect, social worker)	19.2
	Associate professional or technical (eg technician, nurse, building inspector, computer programmer, musician)	16.0
	Clerical/secretarial (eg typist, postal clerk, secretary, telephone operator, computer operator, bank clerk)	25.8
	Craft (eg bricklayer, tool maker, electrician, fitter, motor mechanic)	4.6
	Personal and protective (eg police officer, bar staff, hairdresser, undertaker)	4.7
	Sales (eg buyer, sales assistant, sales representative, credit agent)	3.0
	Plant/machine operator (eg assembly line worker, truck driver, taxi or bus driver)	2.7
	Other occupation	.5

Background variable	Category	Percentage of sample
Whether part of management of the organisation	Yes	40.4
	No	59.6
Contract of employment	Temporary	5.9
	Fixed term	4.6
	Permanent	89.5
Actual hours worked in a typical week in main job	10 or less	2.1
	11–20	7.8
	21–30	9.8
	31–40	45.2
	41–50	28.3
	51+	6.7
Age	18-24	8.0
	25-29	12.6
	30-34	15.6
	35-44	31.0
	45-54	24.7
	55-65	8.1
Trade union or staff association membership	Yes	49.1
	No	50.9
Highest educational qualification	No formal qualifications	9.8
	CSE/GCSE (grades D-G)/NVQ level 1	5.9
	O level /GCSE (grades A-C)/NVQ level 2	20.2
	A levels/NVQ level 3	24.2
	Degree or equivalent	30.3
	Postgraduate or equivalent	9.6
Sex	Male	38.5
	Female	61.5
Average gross pay	Less than £111 per week	7.3
	£111–£130 per week	2.3
	£131–£150 per week	2.2
	£151–£170 per week	2.7
	£171–£190 per week	2.7
	£191–£230 per week	9.8
	£231–£270 per week	13.3
	£271–£340 per week	14.1
	£341–£420 per week	13.4
	£421–£500 per week	12.7
	£501–£600 per week	7.6
	£601–£700 per week	4.9
	£701–£800 per week	2.4
	£801–£900 per week	1.5
	£901 or more per week	3.0

Background variable	Category	Percentage of sample
Number of children of school age or younger	0	59.1
	1	15.8
	2	19.1
	3	4.8
	4	.8
	5 or more	.4
Marital status	Single	25.4
	Married or living as married	63.9
	Separated/divorced	9.8
	Widowed	1.0
Ethnic group	White	93.9
	Black or African-Caribbean	2.7
	Asian	2.6
	Another ethnic group (including mixed race)	.9

Appendix 2

Construction of the variables used in the main path analysis

The table below describes how the variables used in the path analysis were constructed from items contained in the survey questionnaire.

Variable name	Variable type[1]	Description
BACKGROUND VARIABLES		
Company size	Interval	Single item, ranging from 2 = 10–24 employees to 6 = 1,000 or more employees
Establishment size	Interval	Single item, ranging from 1 = fewer than 10 employees to 6 = 1,000 or more employees
Multiple job-holder	Dummy	A single dummy variable reflecting whether the respondent had two or more jobs (coded 1) or not (coded 0).
Sector	Dummy	Respondents were asked whether they worked in a privately owned company, NHS or healthcare, central government, or local government (including the police). Sector was represented by dummy variables in the analysis, where the three categories of public sector were compared against the private sector.
Type of contract	Dummy	Two dummy variables were used to represent type of contract: 1. Whether the respondent was employed on a fixed-term contract (coded 1) or not (coded 0). 2. Whether the respondent was employed on a temporary contract (coded 1) or not (coded 0). Each dummy was compared against respondents employed on permanent contracts.
Type of job	Dummy	Three dummy variables were used to represent job type: 1. Whether the jobs could be classified as being broadly 'blue-collar' jobs (coded 1) or not (coded 0). 'Blue collar' jobs here refers to crafts, personal and protective occupations, and plant/machine operators categories. 2. Whether the jobs could be classified as being broadly 'white-collar' jobs (coded 1) or not (coded 0). 'White-collar' jobs here refers to professional, and associate professional and technical categories. 3. Whether the jobs could be classified as being broadly services (coded 1) or not (coded 0). Services here refers to clerical/secretarial, or sales categories. Each dummy was compared against respondents who were formally employed as managers.
Union membership	Dummy	Whether respondent reported belonging to a recognised trade union or staff association (yes = 1, no = 0).
Age	Interval	6-point scale, ranging from 1 = 18–24 to 6 = 55–65.
Gender	Dummy	Male = 1, Female = 0
Education	Interval	6-point scale, ranging from 0 = No formal qualifications to 5=Postgraduate or equivalent.
Income	Interval	15-point scale ranging from 1 = less than £111 per week/less than £5,721 per year, to 15 = £901 or more per week/£46,801 or more per year.
Management level	Dummy	A single dummy variable where the respondent reported whether they saw themselves as part of management (coded 1) or not (coded 0).
Number of hours worked	Interval	Measured by the number of hours the respondent actually worked in a typical week in their main job.

Variable name	Variable type[1]	Description
Ethnicity	Dummy	A single dummy variable where the respondent reported whether they considered themselves to be white (coded 1) or black, African-Caribbean, Asian, or another ethnic group (coded 0).
Number of children	Dummy	A single dummy variable measured by asking the respondent whether they had any children of school age or younger (coded 1) or not (coded 0).
Marital status	Dummy	Two dummy variables were used to represent marital status: 1. Whether the respondent was single (coded 1) or not (coded 0). 2. Whether the respondent was divorced (coded 1) or not (coded 0). Each dummy was compared against respondents who were married.

ANTECEDENTS

Variable name	Variable type	Description
HR practices	Interval	This variable is a count across 11 items assessing HR practices. For each of the items, participants were asked whether a particular aspect of HR applied in their organisation (coded 1) or not (coded 0). The 11 HR practices assessed were the provision of interesting work; avoiding compulsory redundancy; internal recruitment; involvement practices; opportunities for training; kept informed on how well the company is doing; equal opportunity practices; active steps to prevent harassment or bullying; family-friendly policies; formal performance appraisals; and performance-related pay. Alpha = 0.64.
Direct participation	Interval	Six items asking respondents the extent to which they agree with statements surrounding participation in the design of their work (eg 'I vary how I do my work'). Alpha = 0.71.
Climate	Dummy	Respondents were asked how they would describe the cultural climate in their organisation. The scale included 11 items, with a yes/no response. A factor analysis revealed three dimensions: 'friendliness' (6 items: fair-minded, trusting, public-spirited, ethical, supportive, friendly; Alpha = 0.77); 'dynamic' (3 items: dynamic, forward-looking, creative; Alpha = 0.62); and 'bureaucratic' (2 items: bureaucratic, constraining; Alpha = 0.37). Bureaucratic was dropped from further analysis due to an unacceptably low Alpha reliability. 'Friendliness' and 'dynamic' were treated as dummy variables in the path analysis, where 1 represented a 'yes' response to all items contained in the scale, and 0 for otherwise.
Organisational change	Dummy	Single item where respondents were asked whether their organisation as a whole had been going through any major changes in the last year.

THE PSYCHOLOGICAL CONTRACT

Variable name	Variable type	Description
Psychological contract	Interval	11 items assessing the extent to which the respondent feels the organisation has kept its promises (7 items), treated them fairly (2 items), and how much they trust the organisation (3 items). Alpha = 0.86.

Variable name	Variable type[1]	Description
ATTITUDINAL OUTCOMES		
Commitment	Interval	2 items (eg 'How much loyalty would you say you feel towards the organisation you work for as a whole?'). Alpha = 0.69.
Life satisfaction	Interval	7 items (eg 'How satisfied are you with your life as a whole these days?'). Alpha = 0.79.
Work satisfaction	Interval	Single item ('How satisfied are you with your work?').
Security	Interval	Single item ('How do you feel about your present job security?').
Employment relations	Interval	Single item ('Overall, how would you rate relations between employees and management at your organisation?').
BEHAVIOURAL OUTCOMES		
Effort	Interval	Single item ('How hard would you say you work?').
Motivation	Interval	2 items (eg 'How motivated do you feel in your present job?'). Alpha = 0.70.
Obligation to perform organisational citizenship behaviours	Interval	6 items (eg 'How obliged do you feel to volunteer to do tasks outside your job description?'). Alpha = 0.70.
Intention to quit	Interval	Single item ('How likely is it that you will leave this organisation in the following year?').

1.   Variables used in multiple regression are required to be either interval or dummy (dichotomous) variables. Interval variables are where the intervals between the categories are identical and the categories can be ordered in terms of 'more' and 'less' of the concept in question (for example, age, satisfaction, commitment, etc). Dummy variables are used to convert categorical variables (such as gender, industry type, job type, etc) so that they can be used in multiple regression analyses. Dummy variables typically take the form of (0,1) variables or on/off variables. For example, we could turn gender into a dummy variable by coding male as 1 and female as 0, or vice versa.

Notes on statistical procedures

1. Reliability of variables

It is generally considered that Cronbach's Alpha reliability coefficient, the most popular test of inter-item consistency reliability, represents good internal consistency when the coefficient is above 0.8, acceptable in the 0.7 range, and poor when less than 0.6.

2. Path analysis

The figures in the report are a summary of standard multiple regressions using SPSS for Windows, Version 8. The numbers displayed in boxes lying on the lines running from left to right represent the standardised (beta) coefficients from the regression analysis. All the results shown in the figures are significant at the 0.001 level or better, unless otherwise stated. Where otherwise stated, a 'significant' beta weight ('*') has an associated p-value less than 0.05, a 'strongly significant' beta weight ('**') has an associated p-value less than 0.01, and a 'very strongly significant' beta weight ('***') has an associated p-value less than 0.001. The boxes with arrows going into them are the dependent variables in the regression run.

The labels beneath the dependent variables ('Adj Rsq') stand for the adjusted R-square. The adjusted R-square provides a more conservative estimate of the amount of variance that is explained in the dependent variable by the independent variables. The number of independent variables associated with the regression equation inflates the magnitude of the unadjusted R-square, hence the adjusted R-square corrects for this by taking into account the number of independent variables.

3. Logistic analyses

Logistic analyses were performed in cases where the dependent variable was a dichotomous or categorical variable.

Appendix 3

Zero-order correlations for sector, antecedents, the psychological contract and outcome variables

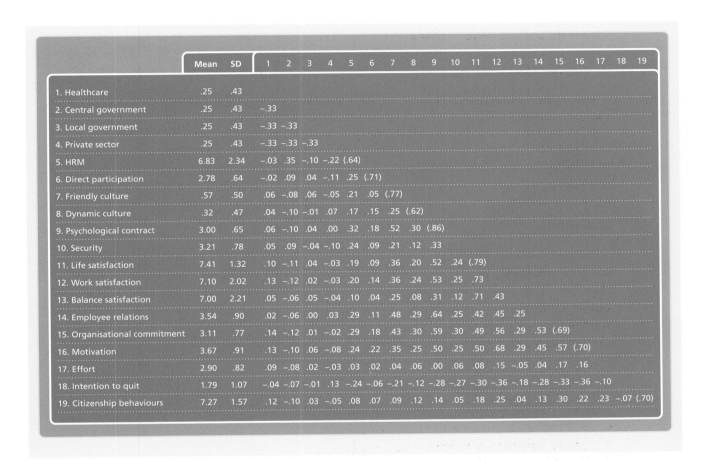

	Mean	SD	1	2	3	4	5	6	7	8	9	10	11	12	13	14	15	16	17	18	19
1. Healthcare	.25	.43																			
2. Central government	.25	.43	−.33																		
3. Local government	.25	.43	−.33	−.33																	
4. Private sector	.25	.43	−.33	−.33	−.33																
5. HRM	6.83	2.34	−.03	.35	−.10	−.22	(.64)														
6. Direct participation	2.78	.64	−.02	.09	.04	−.11	.25	(.71)													
7. Friendly culture	.57	.50	.06	−.08	.06	−.05	.21	.05	(.77)												
8. Dynamic culture	.32	.47	.04	−.10	−.01	.07	.17	.15	.25	(.62)											
9. Psychological contract	3.00	.65	.06	−.10	.04	.00	.32	.18	.52	.30	(.86)										
10. Security	3.21	.78	.05	.09	−.04	−.10	.24	.09	.21	.12	.33										
11. Life satisfaction	7.41	1.32	.10	−.11	.04	−.03	.19	.09	.36	.20	.52	.24	(.79)								
12. Work satisfaction	7.10	2.02	.13	−.12	.02	−.03	.20	.14	.36	.24	.53	.25	.73								
13. Balance satisfaction	7.00	2.21	.05	−.06	.05	−.04	.10	.04	.25	.08	.31	.12	.71	.43							
14. Employee relations	3.54	.90	.02	−.06	.00	.03	.29	.11	.48	.29	.64	.25	.42	.45	.25						
15. Organisational commitment	3.11	.77	.14	−.12	.01	−.02	.29	.18	.43	.30	.59	.30	.49	.56	.29	.53	(.69)				
16. Motivation	3.67	.91	.13	−.10	.06	−.08	.24	.22	.35	.25	.50	.25	.50	.68	.29	.45	.57	(.70)			
17. Effort	2.90	.82	.09	−.08	.02	−.03	.03	.02	.04	.06	.00	.06	.08	.15	−.05	.04	.17	.16			
18. Intention to quit	1.79	1.07	−.04	−.07	−.01	.13	−.24	−.06	−.21	−.12	−.28	−.27	−.30	−.36	−.18	−.28	−.33	−.36	−.10		
19. Citizenship behaviours	7.27	1.57	.12	−.10	.03	−.05	.08	.07	.09	.12	.14	.05	.18	.25	.04	.13	.30	.22	.23	−.07	(.70)

Notes:

Correlations above 0.05 are significant at the 5 per cent level; above 0.06 are significant at the 1 per cent level; above 0.07 are significant at the 0.1 per cent level.

Cronbach Alpha internal reliability coefficients are presented in brackets along the diagonal for variables measured with multiple items.